The Decorated Kitchen

CREATIVE PROJECTS FROM LESLIE BECK

Leslie Beck of *Fiber Mosaics*

Martingale
& COMPANY

Bothell, Washington

That Patchwork Place is an imprint of
Martingale & Company.

Mission Statement
We are dedicated to providing quality products
and service by working together to inspire creativity
and to enrich the lives we touch.

Credits

President: Nancy J. Martin
CEO: Daniel J. Martin
Publisher: Jane Hamada
Editorial Director: Mary V. Green
Editorial Project Manager: Tina Cook
Design Director: Stan Green
Cover and Text Designer: Rohani Design
Technical Editor: Laurie Baker
Copy Editor: Karen Koll
Illustrator: Pat Wagner
Photographer: Brent Kane

Printed in Hong Kong
05 04 03 02 01 00   8 7 6 5 4 3 2 1

Library of Congress Cataloging-in-Publication Data
Beck, Leslie.
   The decorated kitchen: creative projects from Leslie
Beck / Leslie Beck.
      p. cm.
   Includes bibliographical references.
   ISBN 1-56477-350-7
   1. Household linens. 2. Kitchens. 3. Machine sewing.
4. Textile fabrics in interior decoration. I. Title: The
decororated kitchen. II. Title.
TT387 .B43 2000
646.2'1—dc21   00-055401

Dedication

To my husband, Byron Sr., and my children, Christine,
Kate, and Byron Jr. Their belief, support, love, and
patience have given me the strength and encouragement
to pursue a design career.

And, to my readers, I dedicate a cheery, welcoming
kitchen filled with love and friendship.

Acknowledgments

Gratitude and appreciation to my talented staff who
supported me in bringing this book to life:

Byron Jr., who has joined my staff as an artist and
painting style consultant; Retta Warehime, quilt designer,
author, and quilting department supervisor; and Eula
Vance, decorative painter, professional instructor, and
painting department supervisor.

Special recognition goes to my talented quilting and
sewing staff—Debbie Baalman, Shirley Christensen,
Jerrine Kirsch, Gayla Winsor, Shawna Holland, Mary Lou
Larmey, and Lera Beck—and my very talented decorative
painting staff—Linda Alvarez, Linda Leichtfuss, Barbara
Lollar, Barbara Mason, Kathy Renzelman, Kathy Seval,
Ruby Turnbull, and Teresa Houlihan.

Many thanks to Pat Wagner, graphics illustrator, and
Earlene Sullivan, text editor, for their long hours compil-
ing the manuscript.

Thanks to all for the team effort, persistence, and
commitment.

Contents

Preface

The kitchen is the heart of the home. There's no other room where family and friends gather as often or stay as long. Lives are shared at the kitchen table, broken hearts are healed, and laughter, joy, and tears mix together to create generations of memories. When I considered what to include in a kitchen book, I wanted to encompass the kitchen's atmosphere of warm memories and bright tomorrows. I wanted to motivate the reader to dust off and restore old tattered trea-sures and display them (or search flea markets and garage sales for "new" old treasures).

The four kitchen decor collections—Vintage Kitchen, Koffee Klatch Kitchen, Antique Fruit Kitchen, and Folk Art Rooster Kitchen—are the result. Here you will find kitchens with a bright, warm, welcoming atmosphere, kitchens just right for a cup of coffee and a place to sit a spell and share. Enjoy selecting and creating a new look for your heart of the home.

General Sewing Instructions

SUPPLIES

Much like the ingredients you need for many of the recipes you prepare in your kitchen, the tools you need to create the projects in this book are probably already in your sewing "pantry." All you'll need to add is the main ingredient—fabric!

Cutting guides. You'll need a cutting guide to measure fabric and to guide the rotary cutter. There are many appropriate rulers, but one of my favorites is the 24" acrylic type that includes gridded lines for cutting strips, guidelines for marking and cutting 45° and 60° angles, and ¼" increments marked along the edge. A guide such as a Bias Square® is useful for squaring up blocks and for making certain that the ruler is properly positioned on the fabric for rotary cutting. Visit your local quilt shop to choose your own personal favorites from the many options available.

Iron and ironing board. These are essential as you'll want to press frequently and carefully to ensure smooth, accurately stitched results. An experienced quilter may tell you that she spends more time pressing than sewing. Add a Teflon pressing sheet for fusing together appliqué pieces.

Needles. Use sewing-machine needles sized for cotton fabrics, such as 70/10 or 80/12. Keep a sharp needle in the machine. A dull needle interferes with tension and causes skipped, loose, or uneven stitches. In addition, keep an assortment of hand sewing and quilting needles available in sizes such as #8, #9, and #10.

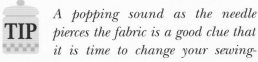

TIP *A popping sound as the needle pierces the fabric is a good clue that it is time to change your sewing-machine needle.*

Pins. Keep a good supply of glass- or plastic-headed pins nearby. Long pins are especially helpful for pinning multiple layers together. A visit to your local quilt shop will help you decide which pins are best for your project.

Rotary cutter and mat. A large rotary cutter enables you to quickly cut the strips and pieces you'll need for most of these projects. A self-healing mat protects both the cutter blade and tabletop.

Sewing machine. You don't need anything fancy: just a reliable straight-stitch machine in good working order. Adjust the stitch length so the stitches hold seams in place securely, but are easy to remove if necessary. Of key importance is the ability to gauge an accurate $\frac{1}{4}$" seam allowance. If you do not have a $\frac{1}{4}$" foot for your machine, contact your machine dealer or local quilt shop for assistance, or mark your machine as suggested in "Machine Piecing" on pages 6–8.

Thread. Use a good-quality, all-purpose 100 percent–cotton, cotton-wrapped-polyester, or polyester sewing thread. Do not use prewaxed hand-quilting thread in your sewing machine.

FABRIC

While it is not necessary to purchase the most expensive fabric, a good rule of thumb in selecting fabric is to buy the best you can afford. Light- to medium-weight 100 percent–cotton fabric produces the best results in any quilting project. Good-quality cotton is reasonably uniform, wrinkle-free, and closely woven with long, fine threads. Avoid poor-quality fabric that wrinkles easily and is uneven or loosely woven with short, weak threads.

Color is a personal choice. The only person to please is you. If you are unsure how to select colors that will look nice together in a finished project, try the "blender technique." A blender fabric is one with four or more colors. Choose a fabric print you really love and use this print as a palette to select additional fabrics. The fabric designer has already done the work of coordinating the colors for you! If you like the colors in the blender fabric and choose those colors for coordinating fabrics, chances are you will be pleased with the finished project.

Arrange your fabric choices on the background fabric you've chosen, and then stand back. Take off your glasses, squint, or use a Ruby Beholder® value-finding tool to see if any fabrics blend too closely. For best results, include a good range of lights, mediums, and darks, and keep each value distinct. If any of the fabrics are too close in value, substitute another fabric until you have the right contrast.

View the scale of the prints in relation to how they will be used in the project. If you need just a small piece in the block, use a small-scale print. A large-scale print is better showcased in a larger piece.

The fabric amounts listed for the individual projects assume that the fabric is at least 42" wide after laundering and pressing.

TECHNIQUES

The following are some basic cutting, stitching, and embellishing guidelines to help you complete the projects in this book.

Rotary Cutting

The pieced projects in *The Decorated Kitchen* do not require templates. You'll rotary cut strips, then crosscut strips into smaller segments and combine them to complete the necessary blocks and units. All rotary measurements include $\frac{1}{4}$"-wide seam allowances, unless otherwise noted.

Note: Reverse the following rotary-cutting techniques if you are left-handed.

1. Fold fabric in half lengthwise, matching the selvages. Place the fabric on the cutting mat so that the length of fabric lies to your right, with raw edges on the left.

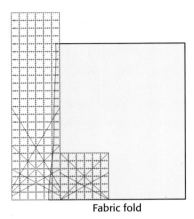

Fabric fold

2. Align a Bias Square ruler with the fold and place a long ruler against it. Remove the Bias Square and press firmly on the ruler to keep it from moving. Place the cutter blade next to the ruler and, exerting an even pressure on the rotary cutter, begin cutting. Always roll the cutter away from yourself! As you cut, move your fingers along the ruler as necessary to hold it steadily in place. After cutting, check to see if all the layers have been cut. If not, try again, this time applying more pressure to the cutter.

3. Keeping the fabric to your right, use the ruler to measure a strip of the appropriate width from the left straight edge. If, for instance, you need a 2½" x 42" strip of fabric, align the fabric edge with the 2½" line on the ruler and cut along the ruler's edge.

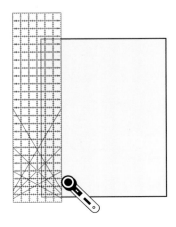

4. Turn the strip horizontally and cut to the desired shape and size.

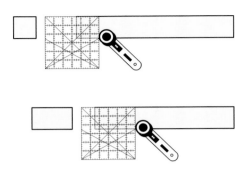

Machine Piecing

Accuracy is important when machine piecing. Unless otherwise noted, use a ¼"-wide seam allowance for all the projects in this book. Move the needle position so that it is ¼" from the right side of the presser foot, or measure ¼" to the right of the needle and mark the seam allowance on the sewing machine with a piece of masking tape. For many of today's machines, you also can buy a presser foot that measures ¼" from the needle to the presser foot outside edge.

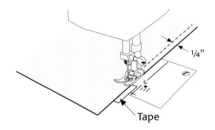

¼"

Tape

Often, you can save time and thread by chain-piecing. Place pieces to be joined right sides together and pin as necessary. Stitch the seam, but do not lift the presser foot or cut the connecting threads; just feed in the next pair of pieces. Join as many pairs as possible, then clip the threads between the pieces.

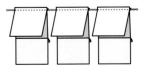

Matching Seams and Points

It is not always easy to line up seams and match points perfectly, especially if you rely on chance! Try these simple techniques to help achieve perfect points.

- Poke a pin into one point along the seam line and through to the seam or other point it must match. Slide the fabric pieces together until the pin is perpendicular to the fabric and the pieces line up. Pin securely on both sides of the point you are matching. Remove the first pin and stitch.

- Whenever possible, work with opposing seam allowances. When matching seam lines for sewing, make sure the seam allowance on the bottom layer is pressed so that it moves easily over the feed dogs, then press the top seam allowance in the opposite direction. This "locks" the seams into position so you can line them up exactly. Pin the seam allowances in place if necessary.

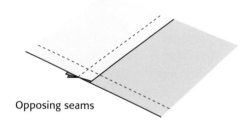

Opposing seams

- If the pieces being joined are slightly different in length, pin the pieces together at the ends and at the seam; then sew with the longer piece on the bottom, against the feed dogs. The feed dogs will ease the fullness on the bottom piece, coaxing both pieces past the needle together.

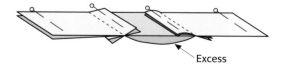

Excess

> **TIP** *For extra-tricky junctions, stitch 1" to ¾" from the intersection and stop with the needle down. Set the sewing machine for a longer stitch length; then continue stitching ¾" to 1" past the intersection. With the needle down, return to the standard stitch length and resume stitching. When you finish the seam, check to see if the points match. If they do, simply restitch over the long stitches. If not, you can easily remove the long stitch, adjust, re-pin, then try again until the points match.*

Angled Piecing

The following methods of sewing angles do not require templates and are more accurate, less intimidating, and even easier than methods that do. Choose your method based upon the direction of the angle or the number of angles in each piece.

When sewing angles, place the pieces right sides together and draw a diagonal line on the wrong side of one of the pieces. Use a fine-point marker or a sharp pencil to draw the line at the angle shown in the project instructions. Sew exactly on the drawn line and cut away the excess fabric, leaving a ¼"-wide seam allowance.

To sew a small square to a larger piece:

1. Draw a diagonal line on the wrong side of the small square.
2. With right sides together, lay the square over the other fabric piece as indicated, making sure the diagonal line lies in the proper direction for your particular unit.

3. Stitch directly on the diagonal line and cut away the excess fabric, leaving a ¼"-wide seam allowance. Press the seam allowances toward the dark fabric unless directed otherwise.

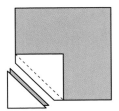 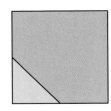

When sewing two or more squares to another piece of fabric, add one square, cut away the excess, and press. Then add the next square, cut away, and press, repeating until you've added all the squares.

To sew a rectangle to a rectangle:

1. With right sides together, lay one rectangle on top of the other at a 90° angle, matching corners.

2. Draw a line at a 45° angle from the corner of the top rectangle to the corner of the bottom rectangle.

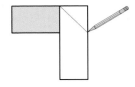

3. Stitch along the diagonal line and cut away the excess fabric, leaving a ¼"-wide seam allowance. Press seam allowances toward the darker fabric unless directed otherwise.

 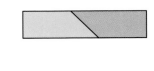

Pressing

Place a freshly laundered, folded towel on the ironing board when pressing blocks. The towel helps ease out any unwanted fullness, so the project will lie flat.

Use a dry iron set on the cotton setting and a spray bottle filled with water to create steam. Using the steam feature on your iron can distort pieces (especially smaller ones) and even alter the block shape because of the temperature and force at which the steam is emitted from the iron. Always test the iron temperature on a scrap of fabric before pressing the project piece to avoid scorching the fabric.

Develop the habit of pressing each seam as it is sewn. Turn the piece to the wrong side and "tack press" by lightly touching the iron to the seam allowance to get it started in the right direction. On the right side, spray lightly with water and press with gentle pressure from the center out. Check the block's wrong side to make sure all seams are pressed correctly before proceeding.

Appliqué

Some of the projects in this book include appliquéd motifs. Full-size patterns are provided for these projects. *These patterns do not include seam allowances.* Refer to the project instructions for positioning the appliqués on the project.

Two methods of appliqué follow. *Note that all appliqué templates are printed in reverse of how the motif appears in the finished project to make them suitable for the fusible-web technique. Be sure to flip over the templates if you plan to appliqué by hand or are using the templates in a painted project.*

Fusible-Web Appliqué

Fusible-web appliqué is a quick, efficient alternative to the hand-appliqué method and gives the finished project a wonderful folk-art look. Each shape is traced directly onto a paper-backed fusible bonding agent, which is applied with an iron to the back side of the appliqué fabric. The shape is cut and the paper removed. Then the fabric shape is heat-bonded to the background block and finished with a decorative hand or machine stitch.

There are many fusible products on the market. Experiment to find the one that best suits your needs, and be sure to read and follow the manufacturer's instructions.

Remember: Because the fusible material is bonded to the wrong side of the fabric, the appliqué patterns for the projects in this book have been printed in reverse. When the shape is flipped over to be bonded to the background, the appliqué appears correctly on the finished project.

TIP *If the base fabric will be seen through the appliqué fabric, apply fusible woven interfacing to the wrong side of the fabric before fusing the bonding agent to the appliqué piece. Be sure to prewash and dry the interfacing before applying it to the fabric.*

1. Trace the appropriate appliqué patterns directly onto fusible material; cut out around the traced designs, leaving a ⅛" margin.

2. Fuse the traced designs to the wrong side of the appropriate appliqué fabric, cut on the drawn lines, and remove the paper backing.
3. When the appliqué involves more than one piece, fuse the pieces together before adhering them to the background. Use a Teflon pressing sheet under and over the appliqué pieces to protect the fabric, the iron, and the ironing surface from the fusible product.
4. Refer to the instructions and finished project photo for guidance in positioning the appliqués in place.
5. Machine stitch the fused design to the background using a blanket stitch or a very short (⅛"-wide) zigzag stitch.

Note: If tear-away stabilizer is required for a project, cut the stabilizer 1" or 2" larger than the appliqué and place the stabilizer between the project and the feed dogs. Typing or other lightweight paper may be used as a substitute stabilizer.

Hand Appliqué

Hand appliqué involves applying (or stitching) a motif to a background block or unit. It is done with an invisible stitch, using matching thread and a small (size #11 or #12), fine appliqué needle.

1. Transfer the appropriate pattern pieces to cardboard or template plastic. *Remember:* Because the patterns are reversed for the fusible method, you will need to turn them over for hand appliqué unless they are symmetrical.
2. Place the template on the right side of the fabric, reversing if necessary, and trace with a sharp pencil. Cut out the shape, adding a ¼"-wide seam allowance. After cutting, clip into the seam allowance on inside curves only.

3. Turn the fabric raw edge to the wrong side on the drawn line and baste with a light-colored thread.

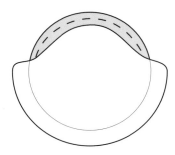

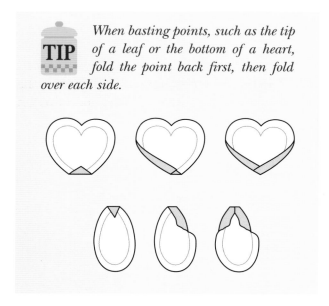

TIP *When basting points, such as the tip of a leaf or the bottom of a heart, fold the point back first, then fold over each side.*

4. Pin the basted motifs in place, referring to the instructions or finished project photo to position the pieces.

5. Appliqué the pieces. Use thread that matches the color of the appliqué.

• Knot the thread and bring the needle up from the wrong side, through the background fabric, barely catching the folded edge of the appliqué.

• Insert the needle into the background fabric beside the folded edge, as close as possible to the place where the thread came through the background fabric. Travel under the background fabric to make a tiny 1/8" stitch; then bring the needle once again through the background fabric and the

appliqué's folded edge. Continue around the perimeter of the shape, making snug, even stitches. Use the point of the needle to turn and smooth the fabric on curved edges.

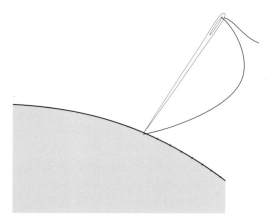

Bring the needle straight back down.

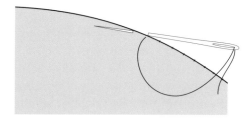

6. Finish with a knot on the wrong side of the appliquéd piece; remove the basting stitches.

Embroidery Stitches

Hand embroidery lends a touch of interest and texture to the finished project. It can also serve a practical purpose by securing an appliqué shape to the background fabric.

Blanket Stitch

This embroidery stitch has recently become popular again as an alternative to machine stitching to finish fusible appliqué. A row of blanket stitches around the edges of fused appliqué pieces gives them a finished look and prevents the edges from peeling up.

If you are planning to hand stitch your fusible appliqué, choose a light- to medium-weight fusible web that a needle can penetrate. Follow the manufacturer's instructions for fusing the appliqué pieces in place. Use a needle larger than you would normally use for hand embroidery and three strands of embroidery floss unless otherwise indicated.

1. Knot the thread and bring it from the wrong side to the right side of the piece, coming out right next to the edge of the appliqué piece at A as shown. Insert the needle through all layers at B and bring the needle out at the edge of the appliqué piece at C. Loop the thread under the tip of the needle.

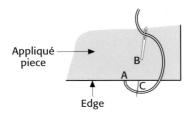

2. Pull the thread through just until snug. The stitches lie close to the edge of the appliqué but should not be so tight that they pull or pucker the piece. Repeat, inserting the needle at evenly spaced intervals for a uniform edge as shown.

Blanket stitch

Feather Stitch

This decorative stitch is worked in the same manner as a blanket stitch but at an angle. The feathers can be stitched in a straight line or curve. It is helpful to work between two guidelines to keep the stitches even.

1. Knot the thread and bring the needle from the wrong side to the right side at A between the guidelines. Take a diagonal stitch to the right at B, slightly below the point where the needle first emerged, and bring it back out at C. Keep the thread under the needle.

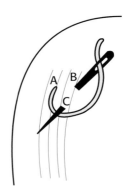

2. Carry the thread to the left-hand side of the guide line. Make a similar diagonal stitch in the opposite direction.

Primitive Running Stitch

This is the simplest and most basic of all stitches. Use it to create detail or to hold layers together. Keep the stitch length and the space between the stitches even for a traditional look, or vary the stitch length for a childlike, primitive look. Knot the thread and bring the needle from the wrong side to the right side at A. Reinsert the needle at B; bring it out again at C.

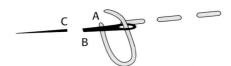

Satin Stitch

Fill in large areas quickly with this easy stitch. Knot the thread and bring the needle from the back to the front at A. Reinsert the needle at the opposite side of the shape you wish to fill at B as shown. Repeat until the desired area is completely covered with long stitches.

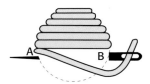

Stem Stitch

This stitch is great for making tiny stems, outlining, or adding detail. Knot the thread and bring the needle from the back to the front at A. Reinsert the needle at B and bring it out again at C as shown. Keep the embroidery floss above the needle as you take each stitch.

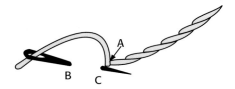

Finishing

The following instructions will help you assemble finished blocks to make a quilt or wall hanging. Some of the techniques described—for example, easy-turn finishing—will also be used to complete various accessories.

Adding Borders

Finished measurements of quilts and wall hangings may vary slightly due to personal cutting and sewing techniques. While specific border measurements are listed for the projects, I recommend that you double-check and adjust border measurements as necessary before sewing borders to your quilt. Carefully matching measurements helps to keep quilts square and avoid rippled borders.

Note: The borders for all projects in this book are straight rather than mitered.

1. Measure the quilt top through its vertical center. Cut side strips to that length. Mark the midpoints of both the side border strips and the quilt top. Place the border strips and quilt top right sides together, pinning to match ends and midpoints. Add additional pins to ease as necessary. Stitch the border strips to the quilt top with a ¼"-wide seam allowance and press the seams toward the border.

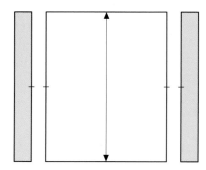

2. Measure the quilt top through its horizontal center, including the side borders. Cut the top and bottom border strips to that length. Mark the midpoints of both the border strips and the quilt top. Place the border strips and quilt top right sides together, pinning to match ends and midpoints. Add additional pins to ease as necessary. Stitch the border strips to the quilt top with a ¼"-wide seam allowance; press the seams toward the border.

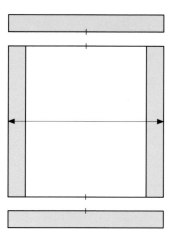

Choosing Batting and Backing

Choosing the right batting and backing for a project is just as important as the selection of fabric for the top. Consider durability, appearance, and the way the quilt will be used, cared for, and cleaned when making your decision.

Personal batting preferences vary. Take time to try different quilting techniques on different types and weights of batting to develop a feel for the look you want and the way the batting handles.

The batting choices for a wall hanging will be different than those made for a bed quilt. For wall hangings, choose a thin batting (100 percent cotton or cotton blend) that will hang flat against the wall. These ultra-thin battings can be machine or hand quilted.

For larger projects, high-loft polyester batting gives a fat, cushiony look. These thick battings are more difficult to needle, but can be machine quilted or tied. Low-loft cotton or cotton-blend batting gives a supple, traditional look, and is perfect for hand quilting.

While muslin is the traditional choice for backing, consider using a single print, or even piecing strips and scraps together until you have a backing of the desired size. Using a variety of fabrics is a great way to use leftovers and to create an interesting quilt back. Consider also whether you plan to machine or hand quilt your work. If you intend to hand quilt, choose a solid or almost solid backing fabric to showcase your beautiful hand stitches, as well as one that allows a quilting needle to glide through comfortably. Do not use bed sheets for your backing since most sheets are difficult to push a needle through.

Cut the backing 4" larger than the size of the finished top. For large quilts, there are 90"- and 108"-wide fabrics available. If it is necessary to piece the backing to get the necessary size, join two or three lengths of fabric as shown and press the seams open.

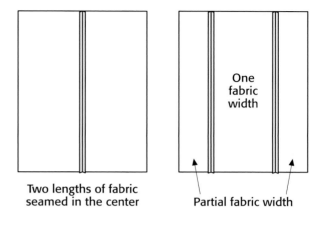

Two lengths of fabric seamed in the center

Partial fabric width

One fabric width

Assembling the Layers

"Sandwiching" is the term commonly used to describe joining the three quilt layers. Begin by laying the backing, wrong side up, on a flat surface, such as a tabletop or floor. Secure it with masking tape around all four edges. Take care to smooth out all the wrinkles, but don't distort it by pulling too tightly.

Next, smooth the batting on top of the backing. Make sure it covers the entire backing. Complete the "sandwich" by laying the quilt top, right side up, on the batting and smoothing out any wrinkles from the center to the outside edges.

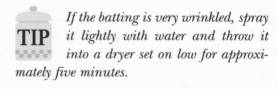

If the batting is very wrinkled, spray it lightly with water and throw it into a dryer set on low for approximately five minutes.

For smaller projects (or those you plan to quilt by machine), pin-baste with 1"-long rust-proof safety pins. Space the pins 4" to 6" apart, working from the center out and avoiding any marked quilting lines.

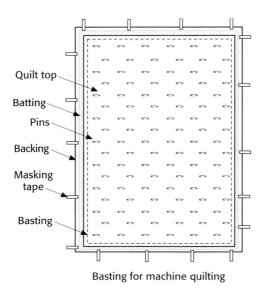

Quilt top
Batting
Pins
Backing
Masking tape
Basting

Basting for machine quilting

For larger projects (or those you plan to hand quilt), hand baste the layers together. Use a long needle and light-colored thread to take large stitches from the center to the quilt's outer top edge. Return to the center, basting to the quilt's outer bottom edge, then to the right and left edges. Continue basting from the center out, creating a star-burst pattern.

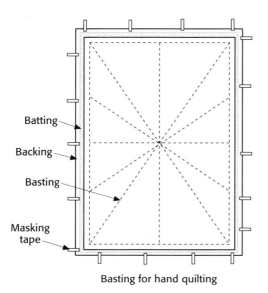

Batting
Backing
Basting
Masking tape

Basting for hand quilting

Quilting

For many of the projects in this book, you will be advised to machine or hand quilt your project "as desired." In the past, most quilts were quilted by hand. Today, quiltmakers have the advantage of choosing either method or a combination of both. Time and the intended use of the quilt are the usual deciding factors.

There are many excellent books to guide you, whether you choose to hand or machine quilt. *Loving Stitches* by Jeana Kimball offers expert instructions on hand quilting. For machine quilting, refer to *Machine Quilting Made Easy* by Maurine Noble. Both are published by That Patchwork Place/Martingale & Co. and are available through your local quilt shop or favorite mail-order source.

When the quilting is complete, remove the pins or long basting stitches and trim the batting and backing to the size of the quilt top.

Finishing the Edges

French Binding

One option for finishing the edges of your quilt or wall hanging is French binding. This binding, constructed from a double thickness of fabric, is attractive, sturdy, and wears well.

Use a ruler and rotary cutter to cut binding strips 2½" x 42". Be sure to cut perfectly straight across the width of the folded fabric. For each project, cut the required number of binding strips and join them with a 45° diagonal seam as described here, using quilting author Mimi Dietrich's technique to distribute seam bulk smoothly over the quilt's edges.

1. Place 2 strips right sides together, crossing the ends at right angles as shown. Lay them on a flat surface and pin.

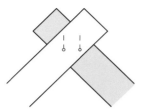

2. Imagine the strips as a large letter A and draw a line across the strips to form the crossbar as shown. Sew directly on the line.

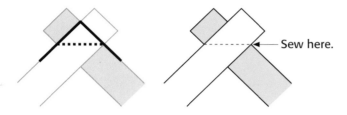

Sew here.

3. Trim the excess fabric, leaving a ¼"-wide seam allowance.

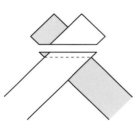

4. Press the seam open.

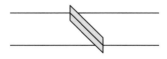

5. Fold the binding strips in half lengthwise, wrong sides together, and press.

6. To determine the length of the top and bottom bindings, measure the width of the quilt through its horizontal center and cut 2

strips to that measurement. Match the top and bottom raw edges of the quilt with the raw edges of the binding, right sides together. Pin, then sew the binding to the quilt with a ¼"-wide seam allowance. Fold the binding over the seam allowance to the back of the quilt and hand stitch in place along the seam line.

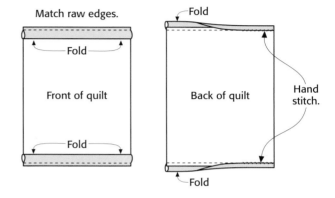

7. For the side bindings, measure the length of the quilt through its vertical center, add 1" to this measurement, and cut 2 binding strips to that length. For a clean-finished edge, fold each end under ½" and press.

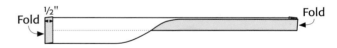

Sew the binding strips to the left and right sides of the quilt, and finish them in the same way as the top and bottom binding were finished.

Easy-Turn Finishing

This simple method is used to finish many of the accessories presented in this book. It also makes a quick, no-fuss finish for quilts and wall hangings. For some projects, batting is not required. Follow the instructions for each project, omitting the batting if necessary.

1. Trim the backing and batting to the same size as the project top. Place the project top

and backing right sides together, with the backing as the top layer. Lay on the batting, carefully smoothing all layers, and pin.

2. Unless otherwise noted, sew around the outside raw edges with a $\frac{1}{4}$"-wide seam allowance. Leave an opening large enough for turning the project right side out.

3. Trim the excess seam allowance as necessary, clip the corners on the diagonal, and turn the project through the opening.

4. Press the project, and slipstitch the opening closed.

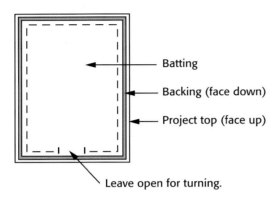

Batting

Backing (face down)

Project top (face up)

Leave open for turning.

General Painting Instructions

Painted kitchen accents are a part of each of the kitchen themes presented in this book. If you're tempted to shy away from them just because you've never painted, don't. Most of the projects are just right for the beginning to intermediate painter. And if you find that you still need help, your local craft store is always a great source of help.

For each project presented, a paint palette and supply list are given. Refer to the project photographs for design placement ideas.

SUPPLIES

Brushes. You'll need brushes in several sizes and types to apply the paint to the project. Polyfoam brushes are ideal for painting base coats in large areas. I find that a 2", 1½", 1" and ½" are the most handy. For more detailed painting, you will need decorative paint brushes in the following types and sizes: #3 Round; #8, #12, and #14 Shader; #2/0 and #10/0 Liner.

Graphite paper. Graphite paper is needed to transfer the pattern to the project. Make the lines clear enough to see, but light enough that the paint will cover the marks.

Miscellaneous accessories. An acrylic paint palette is necessary for holding the paint. You will also need a brush basin or other receptacle to hold water for cleaning the brushes between colors, and paper towels for blotting brushes and for clean-up.

Sanding supplies. Sand the project with a fine sanding disk first. Remove the sanding dust from the surface with a tack cloth. Do the final sanding with a brown paper bag.

Sealer. Set the paint and ink with a matte-finish acrylic sealer.

Tape. Use Scotch Magic Tape to mask off borders, straight lines, and checkerboards.

Tracing paper. Trace the patterns in the book onto tracing paper.

TERMS AND TECHNIQUES

Base coat. A solid application of paint covering the surface or design. Two or three light coats are better than one heavy coat. Sand lightly between coats with a sanding disk or a brown paper bag. Remove sanding dust with a tack cloth. Allow paint to dry between coats, or before painting adjacent areas.

Checkerboards. There are several ways to create checkerboards. Precut stencils are available in many sizes and are a good option for the beginning painter. Purchase stencils to fit the project surface. Let the paint dry before moving the stencil. New kitchen sponges, cut to the desired size, also can be used for checkerboards. Moisten and blot until there is no water left in the sponge. Dip the moist sponge in paint, blot excess paint on a paper towel, then lay the sponge flat on the project. Polyfoam brushes can also be used. They are inexpensive and available in all sizes. Tape off the checkerboard area with Scotch Magic Tape; then use the brush to paint the area.

Dots and dot clusters. Apply paint dots to a surface by dipping a stylus, the tip of a round toothpick, or the handle end of a paintbrush in paint.

Mottle. In this technique, a darker paint color is applied to a lighter base color, then portions of the paint are randomly removed to produce a mottled effect. Mix extender with the desired paint color until it is the consistency of ink. Brush the mixture on the surface. Lay plastic wrap over the wet paint; pull off the plastic wrap. Or, gather the plastic wrap into a wad and tap the wad up and down on the wet paint to remove it.

Outlining. Use a size 2/0 or 10/0 liner brush. Fully load the liner brush by pulling it through the paint, twisting the brush to a point as you pull. Hold the brush as vertical as possible on the surface and lightly pull the brush toward you.

Penstitching. Mock stitching lines can be achieved with paint and a fine liner brush or with a fine-tip permanent marker. Let the painted design dry at least twenty-four hours before penstitching. Let the penstitched project dry twenty-four hours before sealing.

Shading and highlighting. Shade first, then highlight. Shade with a color one value darker than the base coat. Highlight with one shade lighter than the base coat. Wet the brush and blot it on a paper towel until the shine is gone. Then dip about $\frac{1}{3}$ of the brush in the paint and stroke back and forth on the palette until the color is blended. Pull the brush along the design areas to be highlighted or shaded until the colors are soft with no stop or start marks.

Sponging. In this technique, paint is randomly added to another layer of paint with a sponge. Use a natural sponge. Let your eyes tell you how much of a contrast you want between the base color and sponged-on color. Lightly dampen the sponge and squeeze out the excess water. Dip the sponge into the paint, blot it on a paper towel, and bounce the sponge up and down on the desired surface.

Taping. Use Scotch Magic Tape to mask off areas you do not want to be painted or to keep the painted line crisp. Paint, then remove the tape and let the paint dry.

Transferring patterns. Check the pattern against the surface it will be applied to for correct size. If necessary, use a photocopy machine to reduce or enlarge the pattern. Trace the desired design onto tracing paper; then tape the design to the project surface. Slip graphite paper between the tracing paper and surface. Use a pen, pencil, or stylus to mark over the design lines and transfer the design to the surface.

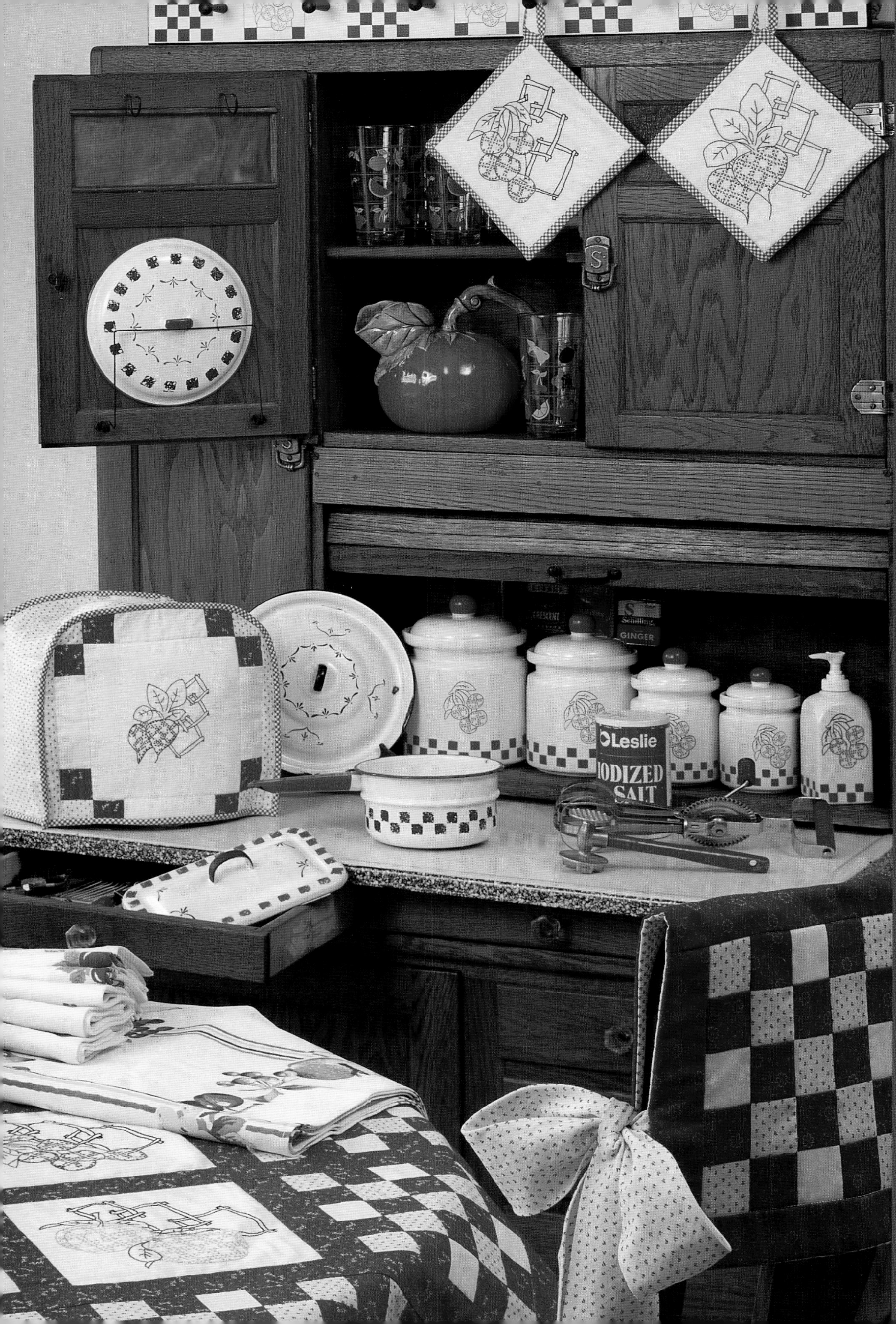
Leslie
IODIZED
SALT
GINGER

Vintage Kitchen

If you have a collection of old-fashioned embroidered tea towels, this is the perfect scenario for using them. Paired with a cheery red-and-white Five Patch block, the embroidered motifs take center stage in this kitchen grouping that's guaranteed to brighten even the most dismal days. Love the design but lack the embroidered motifs? Embroidery patterns are still available at craft and needlework shops. Choose designs approximately 1" smaller than the center square of the embroidered blocks.

THE BASIC FIVE PATCH BLOCK

The following instructions explain how to construct the basic block that will be used to make the stitched projects in this ensemble. The directions for each project tell the length of the strips to cut and how many Five Patch blocks to make.

1. Arrange the red, cream, and white 2"-wide strips together into Strip Sets A, B, and C as shown. With right sides together, pin and sew each strip set. Press the seams in one direction.

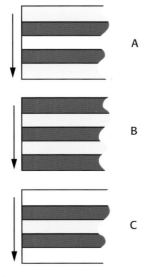

2. Cut each strip set into 2"-wide segments. For *each* block you will need to cut 2 segments *each* from Strip Sets A and B and 1 segment from Strip Set C.

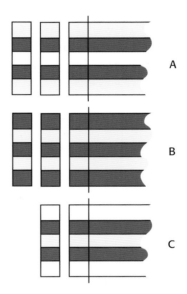

3. Arrange the segments together as shown. Reverse the direction of each segment so the pressed seams are going in the opposite direction of the previous segment. Sew the segments together to complete the Five Patch block. Press the seams in one direction.

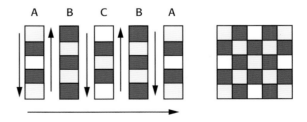

Wall Hanging

Finished Quilt Size 46½" x 39"
Finished Block Size: 7½" x 7½"

MATERIALS (42"-wide fabric)

1¾ yds. red print for pieced blocks, inner and
   outer border, and binding
⅜ yd. cream print for pieced blocks
1 yd. white solid for pieced blocks and middle
   border
10 embroidered tea towels with embroidered
   motifs approximately 3½" square
2½ yds. fabric for backing
Crib-size batting (45" x 60")
5" x 5" square of template plastic

CUTTING

From the red print, cut:
   9 strips, each 2" x 42", for pieced blocks
   2 strips, each 1½" x 30½", for inner side
      borders
   2 strips, each 1½" x 40", for inner top and
      bottom borders
   2 strips, each 3" x 34½", for outer side
      borders
   3 strips, each 3" x 42", for outer top and
      bottom borders
   5 strips, each 2½" x 42", for binding
From the cream print, cut:
   5 strips, each 2" x 42", for pieced blocks
From the white solid, cut:
   5 strips, each 2" x 42", for pieced blocks
   1 strip, 5" x 42", for pieced blocks
   2 strips, each 1½" x 32½", for middle side
      borders
   2 strips, each 1½" x 42", for middle top
      and bottom borders

From the backing fabric, cut and piece:
   1 panel, 43" x 50" (see "Choosing Batting
      and Backing" on page 13)

ASSEMBLING THE WALL HANGING

1. Refer to "The Basic Five Patch Block" on
   page 20 to use the red, cream, and white
   2" x 42" strips to make 1 each of Strip Sets A,
   B, and C. Cut 20 segments each from Strip
   Sets A and B and 10 segments from Strip Set
   C. Make 10 blocks.

2. To make the embroidered block, center the
   5" x 5" square template over the embroidered design on each tea towel. Mark
   around the template outer edges. Cut along
   the marked line.

3. Cut the remaining white 2" x 42" strips into
   20 segments, each 2" x 5". Sew a segment to
   the top and bottom of each embroidered
   square. Make 10 units. Press the seams in
   one direction.

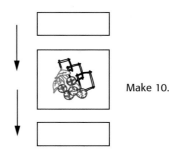

Make 10.

4. Stitch a red 2" x 42" strip to each side of the white 5" x 42" strip. Cut the strip set into 2" segments. Cut 20 segments. Press the seams in one direction.

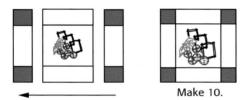

Make 1. Cut 20.

5. Stitch the red-and-white 2" segments to the sides of the embroidered unit from step 3 to complete the embroidered block. Make 10. Press the seams in one direction.

Make 10.

6. Arrange the Five Patch blocks and embroidered blocks in 4 horizontal rows of 5 blocks each. Alternate the block position in each row as shown. Sew the rows together.

7. Refer to "Adding Borders" on page 12 to stitch the inner and middle borders to the quilt top. Stitch the outer border side strip to each side of the quilt top. Press the seams toward the border. Sew the outer border top and bottom strips together end to end to make a single long strip. Cut the strip into 2 segments, each 3" x 47". Stitch the segments to the top and bottom edges of the quilt top. Press the seams toward the border.

FINISHING THE WALL HANGING

1. Layer the backing, batting, and quilt top; baste the layers together (see "Assembling the Layers" on pages 13–14).
2. Quilt as desired (see "Quilting" on page 14).
3. French bind the quilt edges (see "Finishing the Edges" on pages 14–15).

Tablecloth

Finished Tablecloth Size: 46½" x 46½"
Finished Block Size: 7½" x 7½"

MATERIALS (42"-wide fabric)

1⅝ yds. red print for pieced blocks, sashing, and border
⅝ yd. cream print for pieced blocks
⅜ yd. white solid for pieced blocks
9 tea towels with embroidered motifs approximately 6½" square
1½ yds. 60"-wide flannel for backing
8" x 8" square of template plastic

CUTTING

From the red print, cut:
    24 strips, each 2" x 42", for pieced blocks, sashing, and border
From the cream print, cut:
    9 strips, each 2" x 42", for pieced blocks
From the white solid, cut:
    4 strips, each 2" x 42", for pieced blocks
From the backing fabric, cut:
    1 square, 47" x 47"

ASSEMBLING THE TABLECLOTH

1. Refer to "The Basic Five Patch Block" on page 20 to use the red, cream, and white 2" x 42" strips to make 2 each of Strip Sets A and B and 1 Strip Set C. Cut 32 segments each from Strip Sets A and B and 16 segments from Strip Set C. Make 16 blocks.

2. Center the 8" x 8" square template over the embroidered design on each tea towel. Mark around the template outer edges. Cut along the marked line.

3. Cut 4 red 2" x 42" strips into 20 segments, each 2" x 8", for the horizontal sashing strips.

4. Stitch together 2 vertical rows of five Five Patch blocks and 4 horizontal sashing strips each, as shown.

5. Stitch together 3 vertical rows of two Five Patch blocks, 3 embroidered blocks, and 4 sashing strips each, as shown.

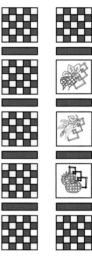

Make 2.   Make 3.

6. Beginning with a 2" x 42" red print strip, alternately stitch together the vertical rows and 2" x 42" strips. Stitch the remaining 2" x 42" strips together end to end. Cut the strip into 2 segments, each 2" x 47". Stitch the strips to the top and bottom of the tablecloth top and bottom edges. Press the seam allowances toward the borders.

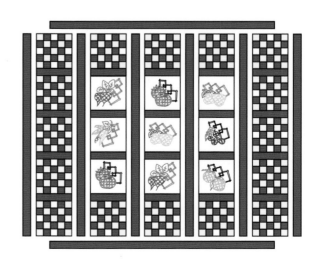

FINISHING THE TABLECLOTH

1. Refer to "Easy-Turn Finishing" on pages 15–16 to stitch the tablecloth top and flannel backing together.

2. Quilt as desired (see "Quilting," page 14).

Valance

Finished size 56½" x 14"

MATERIALS (42"-wide fabric)

1⅜ yds. red print for pieced blocks, borders,
   and lining
⅜ yd. cream print for pieced blocks
⅛ yd. white solid for pieced blocks and lining
4 embroidered tea towels with embroidered
   motifs approximately 6½" square
8" x 8" square of template plastic
Six ½"-diameter decorative buttons

CUTTING

From the red print, cut:
   7 strips, each 2" x 13", for pieced blocks
   4 strips, each 2½" x 42", for side, top, and
      bottom borders
   2 strips, 12" x 42", for lining
From the cream print, cut:
   5 strips, each 2" x 13" for pieced blocks
   6 strips, each 4" x 5½", for tabs
From the white solid, cut:
   3 strips, each 2" x 13", for pieced blocks

ASSEMBLING
THE VALANCE PANEL

1. Refer to "The Basic Five Patch Block" on
   page 20 to use the red, cream, and white 2"
   x 13" strips to make 1 each of Strip Sets A, B,
   and C. Cut 6 segments each from Strip Sets
   A and B and 3 segments from Strip Set C.
   Make 3 blocks.

2. Center the 8" x 8" square template over the
   embroidered design on each tea towel.
   Mark around the template outer edges. Cut
   along the marked line.

3. Beginning with an embroidered block,
   alternately stitch the 4 embroidered blocks
   and three Five Patch blocks together into a
   single horizontal row.

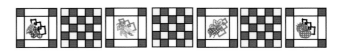

4. Stitch the red 2½" x 42" strips together end
   to end to make a single long strip. Cut the
   strip into 2 segments, each 2½" x 57", for
   the top and bottom borders, and 2 segments, each 2½" x 8", for the side borders.

5. Refer to "Adding Borders" on page 12 to
   stitch the borders to the valance.

LINING AND
FINISHING THE VALANCE

1. Fold each 4" x 5½" tab strip in half, right
   sides together, to make a 2" x 5½" strip. Sew
   1 short end and the long side as shown.
   Trim the excess seam allowance as needed.
   Trim the stitched corners diagonally. Turn
   the tab right sides out, and press.

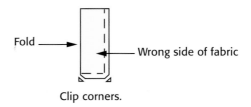

Fold → ← Wrong side of fabric

Clip corners.

2. Space tabs evenly across the right side of the valance top edge. Begin ½" from each end of the valance, and align the tab raw edges with the valance raw edge. Baste the tabs in place with a ⅛"-wide seam allowance.

3. Sew the lining strips together end to end to make a single long strip. Measure the horizontal width through the center of the valance and cut the lining strip to this measurement.

4. Refer to "Easy-Turn Finishing" on pages 15–16 to stitch the valance and lining together.

5. Quilt as desired (see "Quilting" on page 14).

6. Bring the tabs to the front side of the valance, and secure in place with decorative buttons.

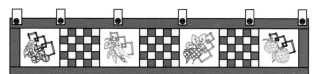

Chair Back Covers

Finished Chair Back Cover Size: 16½" x 36"*
Finished Block Size: 7½" x 13½"

*The size of the chair back cover is determined by measuring the chair back width and front-to-back length. Adjust the cover size to fit your chair back by adjusting the width and/or length of the border strips.

MATERIALS (42"-wide fabric)*

⅞ yd. red print for pieced blocks and borders
2 yds. cream print for pieced blocks, backing, and ties
¼ yd. white solid for pieced blocks
2 yds. of low-loft batting

* Materials given will make two chair back covers.

CUTTING

From the red print, cut:
    13 strips, each 2" x 42", for pieced blocks and borders
From the cream print, cut:
    5 strips, each 2" x 42", for pieced blocks
    8 strips, each 6" x 25", for ties
From the white solid, cut:
    3 strips, each 2" x 42", for pieced blocks

ASSEMBLING THE CHAIR BACK COVERS

1. Refer to "The Basic Five Patch Block" on page 20 to use the red, cream, and white 2" x 42" strips to make 1 each of Strip Sets A, B, and C. Cut Strip Set A into 12 segments, Strip Set B into 16 segments, and Strip Set C into 8 segments. Stitch the segments together as shown. Make 4 blocks.

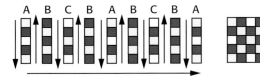

2. From the remaining red print 2" x 42" strips, cut 8 top and bottom border strips, each 2" x 14". If you adjusted the cover finished size, be sure to adjust the width and length of the border strips accordingly.

3. Stitch the top and bottom border strips to the top and bottom of each block. Stitch 2 blocks together vertically. Make 2 block units. Measure the vertical length through the center of each cover, including the border strips. Stitch the remaining 2" x 42" strips together end to end, and cut 4 side border strips to this measurement. Stitch a side border strip to the sides of each cover.

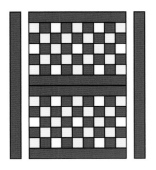

FINISHING THE
CHAIR BACK COVERS

1. Fold each tie strip in half lengthwise, right sides together. Stitch the long raw edge and diagonally across one end. Trim the excess seam allowance as needed. Turn the ties right sides out, and press. Baste across the raw edges of each tie end. Gather the end to 1½" wide, and baste again ⅛" from the end.

2. Measure the chair back covers through the horizontal and vertical centers. Cut two backing and four batting pieces the measured size.

3. Lay each pieced cover on a batting piece and quilt the layers together as desired (see "Quilting" on page 14).

4. Place one quilted top over the chair back. Pin-mark the tie placement on each side of the top, placing the ties equal distance from each end. The placement will depend on the chair and personal preference.

5. Remove the top from the chair and pin the ties in place. Extend the tie gathered end ½" beyond the seam allowance.

Chair back cover shown with coordinating seat pad.

6. Place the backing and quilted top right sides together, sandwiching the ties between the layers. Lay another piece of batting on top of the backing. Pin the layers together.

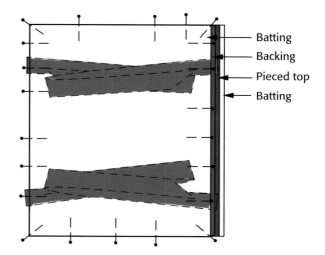

7. Refer to "Easy-Turn Finishing" on pages 15–16 to stitch the quilted top and backing together. Repeat for the second chair back cover.

Chair Seat Pads

Finished Chair Pad Size: 17" x 17"*
Finished Block Size: 6" x 6"

*The chair pad size can be adjusted to a smaller seat by reducing the number of segments in each block.

MATERIALS (42"-wide fabric)*

1⅛ yds. red print for pieced blocks and corner triangles
2½ yds. cream print for pieced blocks, backing, and ties
¼ yd. white solid for pieced blocks
2 embroidered tea towels with motifs approximately 7" square
1¼ yds. of high-loft batting
8½" x 8½" square of template plastic
Pattern tracing paper

*Materials given will make 2 chair pads.

CUTTING

From the red print fabric, cut:
    4 strips, each 2" x 42", for pieced blocks
    4 squares, each 12" x 12"; cut in half once diagonally to make eight corner triangles
From the cream print, cut:
    2 strips, each 2" x 42", for pieced blocks
    8 strips, each 6" x 25", for ties
From the white solid, cut:
    2 strips, each 2" x 42", for pieced blocks
From the backing, cut:
    2 squares, each 18" x 18"

ASSEMBLING THE CHAIR SEAT PADS

1. Arrange the red, cream, and white 2"-wide strips together into Strip Sets A and B as shown. With right sides together, pin and sew each strip set. Press the seams in one direction.

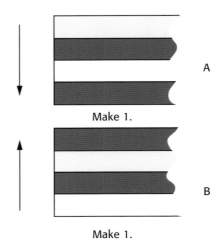

A

Make 1.

B

Make 1.

2. Cut each strip set into 2" segments. Cut 16 segments each from Strip Sets A and B.

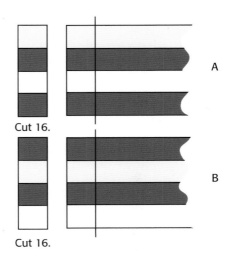

A

Cut 16.

B

Cut 16.

3. Sew the segments together as shown to complete the Four Patch block. Reverse the direction of each segment so the pressed seams are going in the opposite direction of the previous segment. Press the seams in one direction. Make 8 blocks.

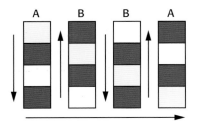

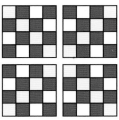

Make 8.

4. Stitch together four Four Patch blocks in the order shown. Position the blocks so the cream print squares run diagonally from corner to corner. Make 2.

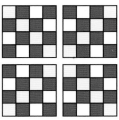

Make 2.

5. With the template placed on point, center the 8½" x 8½" square template over the embroidered design on each tea towel. Mark around the template outer edges. Cut along the marked line. Press under the raw edges ½". Center an embroidered square on each pieced unit from step 4 and top-stitch in place. If the pieced blocks show through the embroidered square, fuse woven interfacing to the back of the square before topstitching in place.

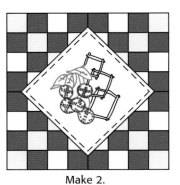

Make 2.

6. Stitch a corner triangle to each side of the pieced block units. Stitch the remaining triangles to the top and bottom edges.

FINISHING THE CHAIR SEAT PADS

1. Lay the pattern tracing paper over the chair seat and trace around the outer edges to make a pattern. Add ¼" to all of the edges for seam allowance.

2. Fold each tie strip in half lengthwise, right sides together. Stitch the long raw edge and diagonally across one end. Trim the excess seam allowance as needed. Turn the ties right sides out, and press. Baste across the raw edges of each tie end. Gather the end to 1½" wide, and baste again ⅛" from the end.

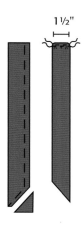

3. Measure the chair seat pads through the horizontal and vertical centers. Cut 4 pieces of batting and 2 pieces of backing the measured size.

4. Lay each pieced top on a batting piece and quilt the layers together as desired (see "Quilting" on page 14).

5. Center the pattern over the quilted top; cut out. Lay pattern over the remaining backing and batting pieces and cut out.

6. Position the pad on the chair seat so the embroidered square is centered. Pin-mark the tie placement at the upper corners of each pad. The tie placement will depend on the chair.

7. Place the gathered ends of 2 ties at each mark. Extend the tie gathered end ½" beyond the seam allowance.

8. Lay a backing piece on each quilted top, right sides together, sandwiching the ties between the layers. Lay the remaining batting layer on top; pin the layers together.

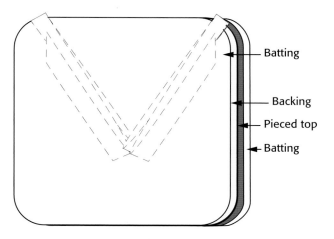

9. Refer to "Easy-Turn Finishing" on page 15 to stitch the layers together.

Hot Pads

Finished Hot Pad Size: 8" x 8"

MATERIALS (42"-wide fabric)*

2 embroidered tea towels with motif approximately 7" square for embroidered hot pad
¼ yd. red print for borders and hanging loops
¼ yd. heat-reflective fabric
¼ yd. thermal fleece
¼ yd. fabric for backing
8½" x 8½" square of template plastic

*Materials given will make 2 hot pads.

CUTTING

From the red print, cut:
  8 strips, each 1" x 8½", for the side borders
  8 strips, each 1" x 9½", for the top and
    bottom borders
  2 strips, each 1½" x 5", for the hanging
    loops
From the heat-reflective fabric, cut:
  2 squares, each 8½" x 8½"
From the thermal fleece, cut:
  2 squares, each 8½" x 8½"
From the backing fabric, cut:
  2 squares, each 8½" x 8½"

ASSEMBLING THE HOT PADS

1. Center the 8½" x 8½" square template over the embroidered design on the tea towel. Mark around the template outer edges. Cut along the marked line.
2. Stitch a side border strip to the sides of each embroidered block and backing square. Press the seams toward the border. Repeat for the top and bottom borders.

FINISHING THE HOT PADS

1. Lay each hot pad top, right side up, on a thermal fleece square. Quilt as desired (see "Quilting" on page 14). Lay each backing square, right side up, on a heat-reflective square. Stitch together as desired.
2. To make the hanging loops, press the 1½" x 5" strips in half lengthwise, wrong sides together. Open the strips and press the raw edges to the center crease. Press the strips in half lengthwise again along the center crease. Topstitch the pressed-under edges together. Fold the strips in half widthwise, aligning the raw edges. Pin the hanging loops to each pieced top at the upper front point.
3. Refer to "Easy-Turn Finishing" on pages 15–16 to stitch the fronts to the backs.

Tea Cozy

Finished size 13" x 10½"

MATERIALS (42"-wide fabric)

Scraps of red print, cream print, and white solid for pieced block
1 embroidered tea towel with motif approximately 7" square for pieced block
⅜ yd. fabric for backing and lining
⅜ yd. of low-loft batting
1 package of red single-fold bias tape for binding
8" x 8" square of template plastic
Pattern tracing paper

CUTTING

From red print scraps, cut:
    8 squares, each 2" x 2", for pieced block
From the cream print scraps, cut:
    4 squares, each 2" x 2", for pieced block
    2 strips, each 2" x 11", for pieced block
From the white solid scraps, cut:
    4 strips, each 2" x 5", for pieced block

ASSEMBLING THE TEA COZY

1. Center the 8" x 8" square template over the embroidered design on the tea towel. Mark around the template outer edges. Cut along the marked line.
2. Stitch a red 2" x 2" square to each end of a white 2" x 5" strip. Make 4.

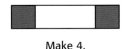

Make 4.

3. Stitch one pieced strip to each side of the embroidered square. Sew a cream 2" x 2" square to each end of the remaining pieced strips. Stitch the strips to the top and bottom of the embroidered square. Sew the cream 2" x 11" strips to the sides of the embroidered unit to complete the block.

4. Trace the tea-cozy pattern on page 117 onto pattern tracing paper. Center the pattern on the pieced block and cut one piece for the front. From the appropriate fabrics, use the pattern to cut 1 backing, 2 lining, and 2 batting pieces.

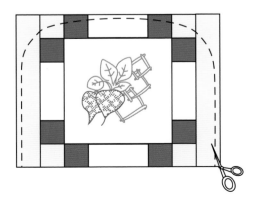

FINISHING THE TEA COZY

1. Layer the front pieces in the following order: lining, wrong side up, batting, and pieced front, right side up. Pin the layers together, and quilt as desired (see "Quilting" on page 14). Repeat for the back pieces, layering the pieces in the following order: lining, wrong side up, batting, and backing.
2. Pin the front and back quilted sections wrong sides together. Stitch along the curved outer edges.
3. Bind the curved edge first, then the bottom edge, with the red bias tape.

TOASTER COVER ADAPTATION

The tea-cozy pattern is easily adapted for a toaster cover. Just measure the toaster width and height and adjust the pattern as necessary. To adjust the pieced block, add additional 2"-wide strips to the sides and/or top and bottom edges if necessary. Cut and assemble the back and front pieces as for the tea cozy. Also cut a gusset piece that measures the toaster width and twice the height plus ½" for seam allowance. Stitch the gusset between the front and back pieces and finish as for the tea cozy.

Canister Set

PAINT PALETTE

Delta CeramDecor PermEnamel: #033 Red Red, #032 Hunter Green

MATERIALS

Ceramic or glass canisters of your choice
Delta CeramDecor PermEnamel Surface Cleaner and Conditioner
Delta CeramDecor PermEnamel Clear Satin Glaze

SURFACE PREPARATION

1. Follow the surface cleaner and conditioner instructions to prepare the surface of the canisters.

2. Use a photocopier to enlarge or reduce the pattern on page 118 to fit the canisters. Center and transfer the design to each one.

PAINTING THE DESIGN

1. Paint a red checkerboard around the bottom of each canister.
2. Outline the cherries and cross stitch design with red paint and the leaves and stems with green.
3. Paint the handles of the canister lids red.
4. Following the manufacturer's instructions, apply clear satin glaze to the surface of the canisters.

Koffee Klatch Kitchen

You can't help but be in a good mood all day long when you begin your day in this inviting kitchen. Set the mood with a wall quilt and table runner made from traditional Log Cabin blocks, and then add an assortment of stitched and painted pieces to complete your colorful ensemble.

THE BASIC LOG CABIN BLOCK

The Koffee Klatch quilt and table runner both are assembled from Log Cabin blocks. The following instructions tell you how to construct the basic Log Cabin block. The directions for each project specify how many Log Cabin blocks to make.

You will need small amounts of seven to thirteen fabrics to make each block: one multicolor print for the center block, three to six red prints and/or solids, and three to six blue prints and/or solids. You should select light, medium, and dark fabrics for each color group.

It is essential to maintain an exact, consistent ¼"-wide seam allowance when constructing the Log Cabin block. Although the sewing is simple, there are many seams. This makes it easy for the block to finish too small or too large if you are not careful!

To help ensure accuracy, each Log Cabin strip for the block is cut exactly to size. Press the seam away from the center of the block as each strip is added; then measure the block. Adjust the seam allowances as needed.

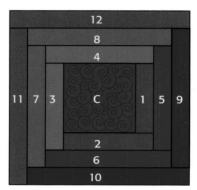

Finished block size: 10"

CUTTING FOR ONE BLOCK

From the multicolor print, cut and label:
    1 square, 4½" x 4½" (C/center)
From the light red prints/solids, randomly cut and label the following:
    1 strip, 1½" x 4½" (#1)
    1 strip, 1½" x 5½" (#2)
From the light blue prints/solids, randomly cut and label the following:
    1 strip, 1½" x 5½" (#3)
    1 strip, 1½" x 6½" (#4)
From the medium red prints/solids, randomly cut and label the following:
    1 strip, 1½" x 6½" (#5)
    1 strip, 1½" x 7½" (#6)

From the medium blue prints/solids, randomly cut and label the following:

1 strip, 1½" x 7½" (#7)
1 strip, 1½" x 8½" (#8)

From the dark red prints/solids, randomly cut and label the following:

1 strip, 1½" x 8½" (#9)
1 strip, 1½" x 9½" (#10)

From the dark blue prints/solids, randomly cut and label the following:

1 strip, 1½" x 9½" (#11)
1 strip, 1½" x 10½" (#12)

ASSEMBLING THE BLOCKS

1. Lay out the entire block as shown.

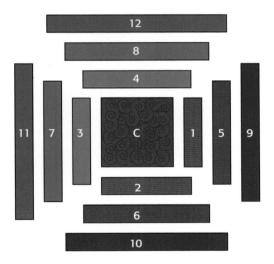

2. Sew #1 to C (the multicolor print center square); press the seam away from the center.

3. Add #2 to the bottom edge of the C/#1 unit and press. Continue adding strips clockwise in numeric sequence around the center square. Press all seams away from the center.

Quilt

Finished Quilt Size: 50" x 59"
Finished Block Size: 10" x 10"

MATERIALS (42"-wide fabric)

⅞ yd. multicolor print for pieced blocks and
   outer border
¼ yd. *each* of 2 light red, 2 medium red, and 2
   dark red prints/solids for pieced blocks
¼ yd. *each* of 2 light blue, 2 medium blue, and
   2 dark blue prints/solids for pieced blocks
1 yd. cream print or solid for setting and
   corner triangles
⅜ yd. blue print for inner border
3¾ yds. fabric for backing
⅝ yd. red print for binding
Twin-size batting (72" x 90")

CUTTING

From the multicolor print, cut:
   2 strips, each 4½" x 42"; crosscut the strips
      into 18 squares, each 4½" x 4½", for
      pieced blocks
   6 strips, each 3" x 42", for outer borders
From the #1 strip fabric, cut:
   2 strips, each 1½" x 42"
From the #2, #3, #4, and #5 strip fabrics, cut
from *each*:
   3 strips, each 1½" x 42", for pieced blocks
From the #6 and #7 strip fabrics, cut from *each*:
   4 strips, each 1½" x 42", for pieced blocks
From the #8, #9, #10, #11, and #12 strip fabrics,
   cut from *each*:
   5 strips, each 1½" x 42", for pieced blocks
From the cream print or solid, cut:
   3 squares, each 15½" x 15½"; cut in half
      twice diagonally to make 12 setting tri-
      angles (you will have 2 left over)

2 squares, each 8¼" x 8¼"; cut in half once
      diagonally to make 4 corner triangles
From the blue print, cut:
   5 strips, each 1½" x 42", for inner borders
From the backing fabric, cut:
   1 panel, 54" x 63" (see "Choosing Batting
      and Backing" on page 13)
From the red print, cut:
   6 strips, each 2½" x 42", for binding

ASSEMBLING THE QUILT TOP

1. Refer to "The Basic Log Cabin Block" on
   pages 42–43 to use the 4½" squares and the
   1½" x 42" strips to construct a total of 18
   Log Cabin blocks.
2. Referring to the diagram below, stitch the
   pieced blocks, setting triangles, and corner
   triangles into 6 rows. Press the seam
   allowances in opposite directions. Stitch the
   rows together.

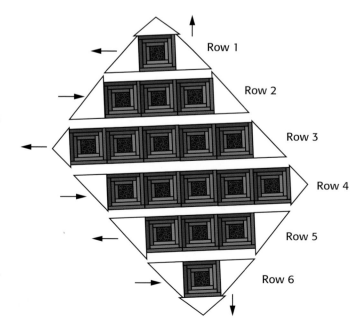

3. Draw a line around the quilt top outer edges ¼" from the pieced block points. Trim along the marked line. Baste ⅛" from the quilt top outer edges.

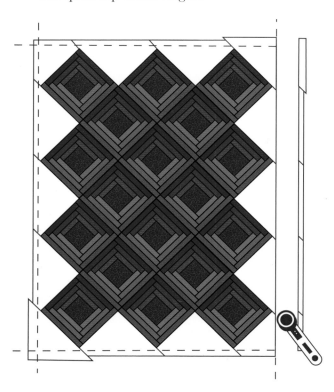

4. Stitch the inner border strips together end to end to make a single long strip. Cut the strip into 2 segments, each 1½" x 57", for the inner side borders, and 2 segments, each 1½" x 45", for the inner top and bottom borders. With right sides together and raw edges aligned, pin and stitch an inner border side strip to each side of the quilt top. Press the seams toward the borders. Stitch the inner top and bottom border strips to the top and bottom edges of the quilt top. Press the seams toward the

border. Stitch the outer border strips together end to end to make a single long strip. Cut the strip into 2 segments, each 3" x 59", for the outer side borders, and 2 strips, each 3" x 50", for the outer top and bottom borders. Stitch to the quilt edges in the same manner as the inner border strips.

FINISHING THE QUILT

1. Layer the backing, batting, and quilt top; baste the layers together (see "Assembling the Layers" on pages 13–14).
2. Quilt as desired (see "Quilting" on page 14).
3. French bind the quilt edges (see "Finishing the Edges" on pages 14–15).

Table Runner

Finished Table Runner Size: 19½" x 50"
Finished Block Size: 10" x 10"

MATERIALS (42"-wide fabric)

½ yd. multicolor print for pieced blocks and
　　outer border
⅛ yd. *each* of 2 light red, 2 medium red, and 2
　　dark red prints/solids for pieced blocks
⅛ yd. *each* of 2 light blue, 2 medium blue, and
　　2 dark blue print/solids for pieced blocks
⅝ yd. cream print or solid for setting triangles
¼ yd. blue print for inner border
1⅞ yds. fabric for backing
⅜ yd. red print for binding
Crib-size batting (45" x 60")

CUTTING

From the multicolor print, cut:
　　3 squares, each 4½" x 4½"
　　2 strips, each 2½" x 42", for outer side
　　　　borders
　　4 strips, each 2½" x 15", for outer end
　　　　borders
From *each* of the red and blue fabrics, cut:
　　1 strip, 1½" x 42", for pieced blocks
From the cream print or solid, cut:
　　1 square, 15½" x 15½"; cut in half twice
　　　　diagonally to make 4 setting triangles
　　4 strips, each 1½" x 12½", for end strips
From the blue print, cut:
　　2 strips, each 1½" x 42", for inner side
　　　　borders
　　4 strips, each 1½" x 15", for inner end
　　　　borders
From the backing fabric, cut:
　　1 panel, 24" x 57"

From the red print, cut:
　　4 strips, each 2½" x 42", for binding

ASSEMBLING THE TABLE RUNNER

1. Refer to "The Basic Log Cabin Block" on
pages 42–43 to use the 4½" x 4½" squares
and the 1½" x 42" strips to construct a total
of 3 Log Cabin blocks.
2. Refer to the diagram below to stitch the setting triangles to the pieced blocks. Press the
seam allowances toward the pieced blocks.

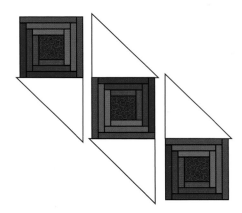

3. Sew the block/setting triangle units
together as shown. Reverse the pressing
direction after each addition.

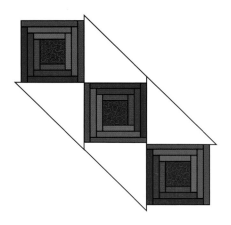

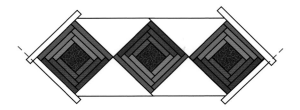

5. Draw a line along each side of the table runner ¼" from the pieced block points. Trim along the marked line, trimming away the excess end strip. Baste ⅛" from the trimmed edges.

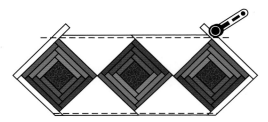

6. Stitch the 1½" x 42" inner side border strips to the sides of the table runner. Trim the ends even with the end strips. Sew the 1½" x 15" inner end border strips to the table runner ends. Trim the ends even with the table runner top after each addition.

4. Stitch a 1½" x 12½" end strip to one side of each end of the table runner. The end strips will extend beyond the sides of the block and setting triangle. Trim the ends even with the block points. The remaining ends will be trimmed away later. Stitch the remaining end strips to the remaining block sides. Trim the ends even with the blocks and end strips.

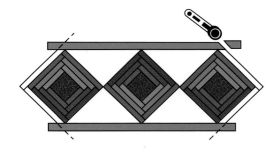

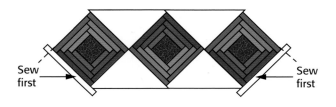

7. Stitch the outer border side and end strips to the table runner top in the same manner as the inner border strips.

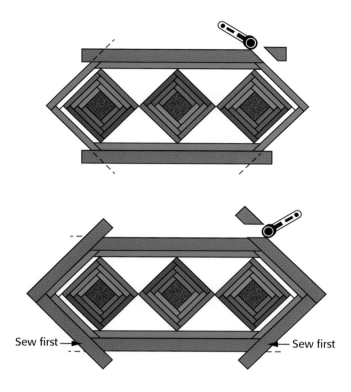

Sew first ➔   ◀— Sew first

FINISHING THE TABLE RUNNER

1. Layer the backing, batting, and table runner top; baste the layers together (see "Assembling the Layers" on pages 13–14).

2. Quilt as desired (see "Quilting" on page 14).

3. Refer to "French Binding" on pages 14–15 to sew the binding strips together end to end to make a single long strip. Press under one end ½". Press the strip in half lengthwise, wrong sides together.

4. Beginning at the center of one long edge, align the binding and the runner raw edges. Begin stitching 2" from the pressed-under end and end stitching ¼" from the corner; backstitch. Remove the runner from the machine.

5. Turn the table runner to prepare to sew the next edge. Fold up the binding to create a 45°-angle fold. With the 45°-angle fold still intact, fold down the binding, having the fold even with the runner upper edge and the raw edge aligned with the quilt side. Beginning at the upper edge fold, stitch until you are ¼" from the next corner. Repeat the folding and stitching instructions to miter the remaining corners.

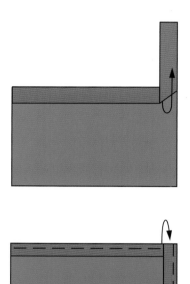

6. End stitching approximately 6" from where you began stitching, and tuck the excess binding inside the beginning of the binding strip. Trim the end so it overlaps the beginning ½". Continue stitching until you reach the point where you began stitching; backstitch.

7. Wrap the binding folded edge to the back of the table runner and hand sew in place, folding the corners so they miter.

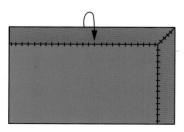

Hot Pads

Finished Hot Pad Size: 9" x 9"

MATERIALS (42"-wide fabric)*

Scrap of multicolor print for pieced block center

⅛ yd. *each* or scraps of 2 light red and 2 medium red prints/solids for pieced blocks

⅛ yd. *each* or scraps of 2 light blue and 2 medium blue print/solids for pieced blocks

¼ yd. red print for border and hanging loops

¼ yd. heat-reflective fabric

¼ yd. thermal fleece

¼ yd. fabric for backing

*Materials given will make 2 hot pads.

CUTTING

From the multicolor print, cut:
    2 squares, each 4½" x 4½", for pieced block
From *each* of the red and blue fabrics, cut:
    1 strip, 1½" x 18", for pieced blocks
From the red print, cut:
    8 strips, each 1" x 8½", for the side borders
    8 strips, each 1" x 9½", for the top and
        bottom borders
    2 strips, each 1½" x 5", for the hanging
        loops
From the heat-reflective fabric, cut:
    2 squares, each 9½" x 9½"
From the thermal fleece, cut:
    2 squares, each 9½" x 9½"
From the backing fabric, cut:
    2 squares, each 9½" x 9½"

ASSEMBLING THE HOT PADS

1. Refer to "The Basic Log Cabin Block" on pages 42–43 to use the 4½" x 4½" squares and 1½" x 18" strips to construct 2 Log Cabin blocks.
2. Stitch a side border strip to the sides of the Log Cabin blocks and each backing square. Press the seams toward the border. Repeat for the top and bottom borders.

FINISHING THE HOT PADS

1. Lay the pieced top, right side up, on the thermal fleece square. Quilt as desired (see "Quilting" on page 14). Lay the backing square, right side up, on the heat-reflective square. Quilt as desired.
2. To make the hanging loop, press each strip in half lengthwise, wrong sides together. Open the strip and press the raw edges to the center crease. Press the strip in half lengthwise again along the center crease. Topstitch the pressed-under edges together. Fold the strip in half widthwise, aligning the raw edges. Pin the hanging loop to the pieced top at the upper front point.
3. Refer to "Easy-Turn Finishing" on pages 15–16 to stitch the quilted front and back pieces together. Repeat for the second hot pad.

Tea Towels

MATERIALS*

2 purchased cotton tea towels
⅜ yd. or scraps of coordinating fabric for the
    borders
⅝ yd. of coordinating rickrack for *each* towel

*Materials given will make 2 tea towels.

CUTTING

From the coordinating fabric, cut:
    2 strips, each 5" wide and ½" longer than
        the width of each tea towel
From the coordinating rickrack, cut:
    2 pieces of rickrack, each 1" longer than
        the width of each tea towel

ASSEMBLING THE TEA TOWELS

1. Press under the long edges of each coordi-
    nating fabric strip ½".

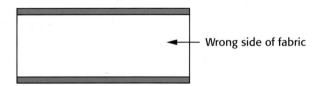

Wrong side of fabric

2. With right sides together, fold the strips in
    half lengthwise. Stitch across each end.
    Turn the strips to the right side and press.

Wrong side of fabric

3. Lay the pressed-under edges of each strip
    over the lower ½" of a tea towel. Topstitch
    through all layers along the pressed-under
    edge.

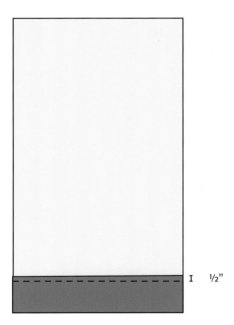

½"

4. Fold under each end of the rickrack ½".
    Position the rickrack over the topstitched
    seam between the coordinating strip and
    tea-towel edge. Align the folded ends of the
    rickrack with the sides of the towel. Stitch
    the rickrack in place. Repeat for the second
    tea towel.

Window Treatment

MATERIALS

Valance fabric in the amount calculated in step 1 of "Calculating Fabric Requirements"

Lining fabric in the amount calculated in step 1 of "Calculating Fabric Requirements"

Curtain fabric in the amount calculated in step 2 of "Calculating Fabric Requirements"

CALCULATING FABRIC REQUIREMENTS

1. To calculate the yardage required for the valance and valance lining fabrics, measure the width of the window to be covered and divide by 14. Round up to the nearest whole number. This will be the number of 20½" finished squares you will need to make. You can make 2 squares from ¾ yard of fabric. For example, if your window measures 36" wide, divide 36 by 14 for a total of 2.5. Round up to 3. You will need 3 squares, each 20½". Purchase 1½ yards each of lining and valance fabric.

2. To calculate the yardage required for the curtain fabric, measure the window width and the desired curtain length. You will need a piece of fabric twice the window width and 6¾" longer than the finished length. For example, if your window measures 36" wide and your desired curtain length is 24", you will need a piece of fabric 72" wide and 30¾" long, or 2 yards.

CUTTING AND ASSEMBLING THE VALANCE PANELS

1. From the valance and lining fabrics *each*, cut the number of squares calculated in step 1 of "Calculating Fabric Requirements."

2. With right sides together, sew a valance and lining square together. Leave an opening for turning. Turn the valance to the right side, and press. Slipstitch the opening closed. Topstitch around the outer edges. Repeat for the remaining valance and lining squares.

CUTTING AND ASSEMBLING THE CURTAIN

1. Cut the curtain fabric to the length and width determined in step 2 of "Calculating Fabric Requirements."

2. Press under the side edges ¼" twice and topstitch in place.

3. Press under the lower edge 2" twice, and topstitch in place.

4. Press under the upper edge ¼". Press under 2½" from the folded edge and topstitch in place.

Watering Can

PAINT PALETTE

DecoArt Americana: #DA170 Santa Red
Delta Ceramcoat: #2504 Yellow, #2089 Navy
Blue, Metal Primer

MATERIALS

Galvanized watering can
Matte-finish acrylic sealer

PREPARING THE WATERING CAN

1. Wash the watering can with a 50 percent
    vinegar/50 percent water mixture. Rinse
    with clean water; dry with a clean cloth.
2. Following the metal primer instructions,
    prime the watering can outer surface.

PAINTING THE WATERING CAN

1. Select a base-coat color from the palette and
    paint the watering can body. Paint the
    handle and spout in a contrasting color.
2. Using the remaining paint color, paint the
    top of the watering can and add a single
    checkerboard border to the watering can
    lower edge. Transfer the motifs on page 118
    to the area directly above the checkerboard
    border and to the upper edge of the water-
    ing can. Make the dots with a stylus or a
    brush handle.

3. Following the manufacturer's instructions,
    apply sealer to the watering can painted
    surface.

Canister Set

PAINT PALETTE

DecoArt Ultra Gloss: #DG30 True Blue, #DG10 Christmas Red
Delta PermEnamel: #029 Ultra White

MATERIALS

Canister jars
Delta PermEnamel Surface Cleaner and
    Conditioner
Delta PermEnamel Clear Satin Glaze

PREPARING THE CANISTERS

1. Using a mild dishwashing soap, wash the canisters; rinse with clean water and dry with a clean cloth.
2. Following the manufacturer's instructions, apply the surface cleaner and conditioner.

PAINTING THE CANISTERS

1. Paint one side of each canister with a white base coat. Apply additional coats until the surface is opaque. Let each coat dry before applying the next coat.
2. Transfer the "Coffee" and "Tea" patterns on page 118 to the bottom of the white area. Paint the letters red.
3. Draw a $9\frac{1}{4}$" square above the painted words. Divide the square into $\frac{1}{4}$" segments for the checks. Paint the checkerboard pattern blue and white.
4. Following the manufacturer's instructions, seal the painted surface with clear satin glaze.

Antique Fruit Kitchen

An apple a day keeps the doctor away. If the old saying is true, you'll never get sick of this fruit-inspired kitchen theme! Subtle colors provide a calming atmos-phere, while painted furniture takes the spotlight. The painting projects are for the advanced intermediate to experienced painter, but be creative and scale down the project to fit your expertise.

Quilt

Finished Quilt Size: 38" x 46"
Finished Block Size: 4" x 4"

MATERIALS (42"-wide fabric)

1¾ yds. cream print for pieced blocks and
    outer border
½ yd. green print for pieced blocks
½ yd. *total* of assorted red prints for pieced
    blocks
¾ yd. dark red print for inner border and
    binding
⅛ yd. *each* or scraps of assorted red and green
    prints and solids for border appliqués
1½ yds. fabric for backing
Embroidery thread: brown, green, red
½ yd. of paper-backed fusible web

CUTTING INSTRUCTIONS

From cream print, cut:
    3 strips, each 2½" x 42", for Irish Chain
        blocks
    4 strips, each 1½" x 42", for Irish Chain
        blocks
    2 strips, each 3½" x 42"; crosscut into 62
        segments, each 1" x 3½", for Apple
        block side borders
    2 strips, each 4½" x 42"; crosscut into 62
        segments, each 1" x 4½", for Apple
        block top and bottom borders
    3 strips, each 1" x 42"; crosscut into 124
        squares, each 1" x 1", for Apple blocks
    2 strips, 1½" x 42"; crosscut into 31 rectan-
        gles, each 1" x 1½", for Apple blocks
    4 strips, each 4½" x 42" for outer borders
From the green print, cut:
    6 strips, 1½" x 42", for Irish Chain blocks
    2 strips, 2½" x 42", for Irish Chain blocks
From the assorted red prints, cut a *total* of :
    31 rectangles, each 3" x 3½", for Apple
        block bottom

62 rectangles, each 1" x 2", for Apple block top (cut two to match each color of 3" x 3½" rectangle)

From the dark red print, cut:

2 strips, each 1½" x 36½", for inner side borders

2 strips, each 1½" x 30½", for inner top and bottom borders

5 strips, each 2½" x 42", for binding

ASSEMBLING THE BLOCKS

1. To make the Irish Chain blocks, arrange the cream and green 2½" x 42" and 1½" x 42" strips together into Strip Sets A and B as shown. With right sides together, pin and sew each strip set. Press the seams toward the green strips. Make 3 of Strip Set A and 2 of Strip Set B. Cut Strip Set A into 64 segments, each 1½" wide. Cut Strip Set B into 32 segments, each 2½" wide.

1½"

A

Cut 64.

2½"

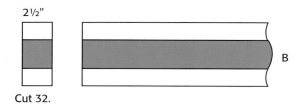

B

Cut 32.

2. Sew the segments together as shown to complete the Irish Chain block. Position each segment so the pressed seams are going in the opposite direction of the previous segment. Press the seam allowance in one direction. Make 32 blocks.

A   B   A

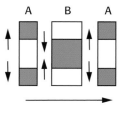

Make 32.

3. To make the Apple block tops, refer to "Angled Piecing" on page 7 to stitch together 2 cream 1" x 1" squares, 1 cream 1" x 1½" rectangle, and 2 red 1" x 2" rectangles as shown. Make 31 Apple block tops.

1" x 1"   1" x 1½"   1" x 2"   1" x 1"

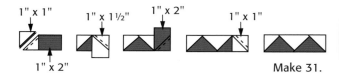

1" x 2"   Make 31.

4. To make the Apple block bottoms, refer to "Angled Piecing" on page 7 to stitch 1 cream 1" x 1" square to each lower corner of a red 3" x 3½" rectangle. Make 31 Apple block bottoms.

3½"

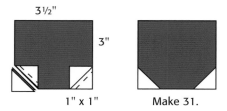

3"

1" x 1"   Make 31.

5. Stitch the Apple block tops and bottoms together. Press the seam allowance toward the block bottom.

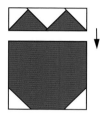

6. Stitch the Apple block side borders to the sides of each Apple block. Press the seam allowances toward the border. Sew the Apple block top and bottom borders to the top and bottom edges of each block. Press the seam allowances toward the border.

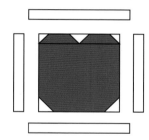

7. Transfer the stem pattern on page 118 to the center of the Apple block top. Satin stitch the stem in place with 2 strands of brown embroidery floss (see "Embroidery Stitches" on pages 10–12). Make 31 blocks.

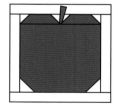

Make 31.

ASSEMBLING THE QUILT TOP

1. Arrange the Irish Chain blocks and Apple blocks in 9 horizontal rows of 7 blocks each. Alternate the block position in each row as shown. Sew the rows together.

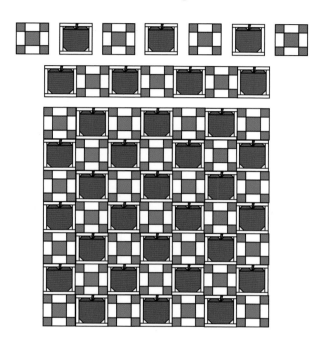

2. Referring to "Adding Borders" on page 12, stitch the inner borders to the quilt top.

3. Use the pattern pieces on page 118 to trace appliqué pieces A through E. Refer to the instructions for "Fusible-Web Appliqué" on page 9 to prepare, cut, and fuse the appliqués in place on the outer border strips. You will need to trace and cut 20 each of A, B, and C; 50 of D; and 60 of E. Refer to the pattern on page 118 to assemble the motifs for each cluster. Because the borders are cut longer than the length and width of the quilt to allow for take-up when stitching, place the motifs an equal distance from each other, leaving enough on the ends to be trimmed later. Machine blanket stitch the motifs in place. If you prefer, you may hand appliqué the motifs (see "Hand Appliqué" on pages 9–10). Stem stitch the vines with two strands of green embroidery floss (see "Embroidery Stitches" on pages 10–12).

4. Trim the border strips to 38½", leaving an equal amount of blank space on each end. Refer to "Adding Borders" on page 12 to stitch the outer borders to the quilt top.

FINISHING THE QUILT

1. Layer the backing, batting, and quilt top; baste the layers together (see "Assembling the Layers" on pages 13–14).
2. Quilt as desired (see "Quilting" on page 14).
3. French bind the quilt edges (see "Finishing the Edges" on pages 14–15).

Window Treatment

MATERIALS

Valance fabric in the amount calculated in step 1 of "Calculating Materials"

Valance lining fabric in the amount calculated in step 1 of "Calculating Materials"

Curtain and valance tie fabric in the amount calculated in step 2 of "Calculating Materials"

Curtain lining fabric in the amount calculated in step 2 of "Calculating Materials"

Fusible woven interfacing in the amount calculated in step 3 of "Calculating Materials"

Size 4 (½" diameter) grommets in the amount calculated in step 4 of "Calculating Materials"

Café-style curtain rod to fit window

CALCULATING MATERIALS

1. To calculate the yardage required for the valance and valance lining fabric, measure the width of the window to be covered and multiply by 2. You will need a strip 12" long by the width calculated. For example, if your window measures 36" wide, multiply 36 by 2 for a total of 72". You can cut up to 3 valance sections from a 42"-wide fabric and piece them together for the desired width.

2. To calculate the yardage required for the curtain and curtain lining fabric, measure the window width. You will need 2 pieces of fabric the width calculated and the length desired plus ½". For example, if your window measures 36" wide and your desired curtain length is 24", you will need 2 pieces of fabric 36" wide and 24½" long. To calculate the additional curtain fabric needed for the valance ties, refer to step 1 to calculate the valance finished width. Add 12" to the

measurement. Divide this number by the fabric width. Round up to the nearest whole number to get the number of strips to cut. Multiply that number by 3.25 and round up to the nearest ⅛ yard for the amount of additional fabric to purchase. For instance, if the finished valance measured 72" wide, you would cut 2 strips, each 3¼" wide (72 + 12 = 84 ÷ 42 = 2 x 3.25 = 6.5"). Purchase ¼ yard of additional curtain fabric.

3. To calculate the interfacing amount required, add the width of the valance and curtain pieces together. Divide this number by the interfacing width. Round this number up to the nearest whole number to get the number of strips to cut. Multiply that number by 3" for the amount of interfacing to purchase. For instance, if the valance and curtain width each measured 72" and your interfacing was 22" wide, you would cut 7 strips, each 3" wide (72 + 72 = 144 ÷ 22 = 6.5. 7 strips x 3" = 21"). Purchase ¾ yard of interfacing.

4. To calculate the number of grommets required, add the width of the valance and curtain pieces together and divide by 5. For instance, if the valance and curtain each measure 72", you will need 29 grommets.

CUTTING AND ASSEMBLING THE VALANCE

1. From the valance and valance lining fabrics *each,* cut a piece of fabric 12" long and the width calculated in step 1 of "Calculating Materials." Piece the fabric together if necessary to make a single strip.

2. On the valance panel wrong side, fuse interfacing strips along the upper edge, leaving ¼" at the top and sides. Butt the interfacing strips together end to end to achieve the length needed.

3. Refer to "Easy-Turn Finishing" on page 15 to stitch the valance and valance lining pieces together.

4. Apply the grommets to the valance upper edge, beginning ½" from the side and upper edges. Space the grommets approximately 5" apart.

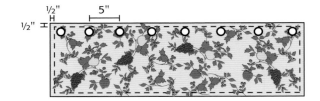

5. Refer to step 2 of "Calculating Materials" to cut the required number of 3¼" tie strips from the remaining curtain fabric. Press each strip in half lengthwise, wrong sides together. Open the strip and press the raw edges to the center crease. Press the strip in half lengthwise again along the center crease. Topstitch the pressed-under edges together.

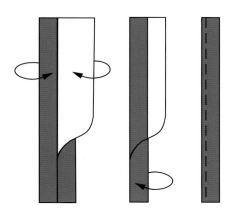

6. Weave the strip through the grommets and over the upper edges as shown. Leave approximately 6 free at each end. Insert the curtain rod under the tie strip. Hang the valance, and tie a bow at each end of the strip.

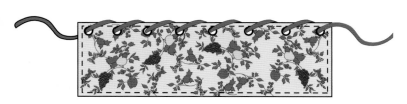

CUTTING AND ASSEMBLING THE CURTAIN

1. Cut the curtain and curtain lining fabric panels to the length and width determined in step 2 of "Calculating Materials."
2. Assemble each panel in the same manner as the valance, omitting the tie instructions.
3. To hang, insert the curtain rod through the grommets.

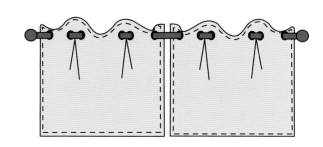

Tote Bag

MATERIALS (42"-wide fabric)*

One pre-printed fabric panel with fruit motifs for front center block

½ yd. dark red solid for inner and outer borders

1 yd. red print for middle border, back, and handles

1 yd. of fabric for lining

¾ yd. low-loft cotton batting

*Materials required are based on a fabric panel approximately 13" x 13". Adjust the other fabric amounts accordingly if your panel measures differently.

CUTTING AND ASSEMBLING THE TOTE BAG PIECES

1. Refer to "Adding Borders" on page 12 to measure the center front panel and cut 1½"- wide inner border strips for the sides, top, and bottom edges from the dark red solid. Stitch the strips to the panel. In the same manner cut and stitch 3½"-wide middle border strips from the red print; stitch to the inner border strips. Repeat to cut 1"-wide outer border strips from the dark red solid for the sides and bottom edges. Do not cut a strip for the top edge. Stitch the strips to the middle border strips.

2. Measure the tote bag top through its vertical and horizontal centers. Cut 1 back, 2 lining, and 2 batting pieces from the appropriate fabrics. Also from the red print, cut 2 strips, each 6" x 10½", for the handles.

3. Lay the pieced top, right side up, on a batting piece and quilt the layers together as desired (see "Quilting" on page 14).

4. Lay the back, right side up, on the remaining batting piece. Pin the back and batting piece to the pieced top, right sides together. Stitch the pieced top to the back along the side and bottom edges. Turn the bag to the right side and press.

5. Press each 6" x 10½" handle strip in half lengthwise, wrong sides together. Open the strip and press the raw edges to the center crease. Press the strip in half lengthwise again along the center crease. Topstitch along the long edges.

6. Position the handles on the right sides of the bag front and back 5½" from each side seam. Align the handle raw edges with the bag raw upper edges. Baste the handles in place.

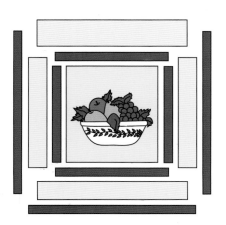

7. Stitch the bag lining pieces right sides together along the sides and lower edge. Leave an opening along one side for turning.

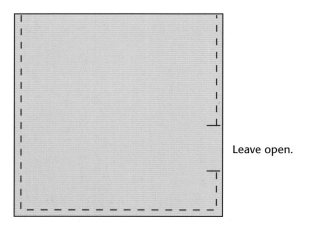

Leave open.

8. Place the bag front/back piece inside the lining with the bag and lining right sides together. Pin together along the upper edge. Match the side seams. Stitch along the upper edge. Backstitch as you stitch across each handle end to reinforce the area.

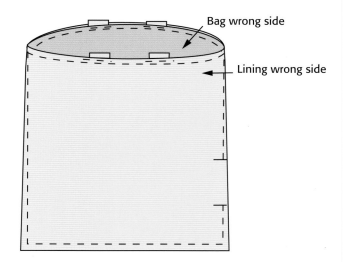

Bag wrong side

Lining wrong side

9. Turn the bag to the right side through the lining side opening. Slipstitch the opening closed. Topstitch the bag upper edge.

Place Mats and Napkins

Place Mat Finished Size: 18" x 14½"
Napkin Finished Size: 15" x 15"

MATERIALS (42"-wide fabric)*

¾ yd. multicolor print for place mat center
    rectangles and napkin squares
¾ yd. dark red print for inner borders and
    binding
⅞ yd. tan print for outer borders and backing
18½" x 30" rectangle of batting

*Materials given will make 2 place mats and 2 napkins.

CUTTING

From the multicolor print, cut:
    2 rectangles, each 9" x 12½", for place
        mats
    2 squares, each 10½" x 10½", for napkins
From the dark red print, cut:
    4 strips, each 1" x 9", for place mat inner
        side borders
    4 strips, each 1" x 13½", for place mat
        inner top and bottom borders
    4 strips, each 2½" x 42", for place mat
        binding
    4 strips, each 3" x 10½", for napkin side
        borders
    4 strips, each 3" x 15½", for napkin top
        and bottom borders
From the tan print, cut:
    4 strips, each 3" x 10", for place mat outer
        side borders
    4 strips, each 3" x 18½", for place mat
        outer top and bottom borders
    2 rectangles, each 18½" x 15", for place
        mat backing

From the batting, cut:
    2 rectangles, each 18½" x 15", for place
        mats

CONSTRUCTING THE PLACE MATS

1. Refer to "Adding Borders" on page 12 to
    stitch the place mat inner and outer border
    strips to each place mat rectangle.

2. For each place mat, layer the backing, bat-
    ting, and place mat top; baste the layers
    together (see "Assembling the Layers" on
    pages 13–14).
3. Quilt as desired (see "Quilting" on page
    14).
4. French bind the quilt edges (see "Finishing
    the Edges" on pages 14–15).

CONSTRUCTING THE NAPKINS

1. Refer to "Adding Borders" on page 12 to stitch the napkin borders to each napkin square. Press under the border raw edges ½". Fold the pressed-under edge to the border seam line. Fold the sides first, then the top and bottom edges. Press in place.

2. From each napkin right side, stitch in the ditch of the border seam, catching the border's pressed-under edge.

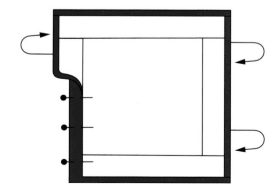

Painted Table

ACRYLIC PAINT PALETTE

DecoArt Americana: #DA3 Buttermilk, #DA164 Light Buttermilk, #DA157 Black Green, #DA168 Golden Straw, #DA172 Black Plum, #DA184 French Vanilla

Delta Ceramcoat: #2484 Black Cherry, #2435 Trail Tan, #2065 Apple Green, #2010 Forest Green, #2495 Cinnamon, #2002 Antique Gold, #2425 Territorial Beige, #2047 Lavender, #2035 Flesh Tan, #2422 Leprechaun, #2062 Maple Sugar Tan, #2447 Village Green

Plaid Folk Art: #957 Burgundy, #420 Linen, #638 Purple Passion, #645 Basil

MATERIALS

Unfinished wood table
Matte-finish varnish
Wood sealer
Plastic wrap
Acrylic paint extender
Natural sea sponge

PREPARING THE SURFACE

1. Lightly sand the surface. Wipe with a tack cloth.
2. Seal with wood sealer.

PAINTING THE TABLE

1. Paint a base coat with Buttermilk.
2. Tape off a 3"-wide border on the table outer edge.

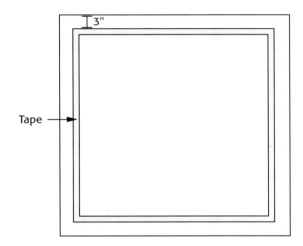

3. Paint the outer border Leprechaun. Mix Village Green with extender and use the sea sponge to mottle the outer border. Let dry. Mix Black Green with extender and use the sea sponge to mottle the outer border lightly. Remove tape.
4. Mix Flesh Tan with the extender. Use the sea sponge to mottle the center square.
5. Paint a 2" checkerboard on the inside border, alternating Buttermilk and French Vanilla. Shade with Maple Sugar Tan on French Vanilla only.
6. Tape off a ¼"-wide border on each side of the checkerboard border. Paint Black Green.
7. Using the patterns on page 119, transfer the fruit designs to the center square as desired. Refer to the Fruit Color Chart on page 77 to paint each fruit.

8. Paint the sides of the table and the legs with Black Green. Apply varnish to the entire table to seal the paint.

Fruit Color Chart

Fruit Name	Base Coat	Shade	Highlight
Dark Apple	Burgundy	Black Cherry	Linen
Light Apple	Antique Gold	Burgundy	Apple Green
Plum	Black Cherry	Black Plum	Linen
Cherry	Burgundy	Black Cherry	Territorial Beige
Dark Pears	Antique Gold	Cinnamon	Linen
Light Pears	Maple Sugar Tan	Cinnamon	Linen
Grapes	Lavender	Purple Passion/ Black Plum mix	Apple Green/ Light Buttermilk mix
Blossoms	Light Buttermilk	Cinnamon	
Large Leaves	Leprechaun	Purple Passion	Basil
Small Leaves	Leprechaun	Black Green	Antique Gold
Vines	Leprechaun	Purple Passion or Black Green	Antique Gold or Basil

PAINTED FURNITURE VARIATIONS

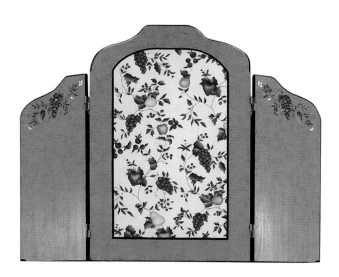

Use the same color palette as for the painted table to add other painted furniture to your kitchen collection. Refer to the photos for inspiration and use the patterns on pages 118 and 119 as desired.

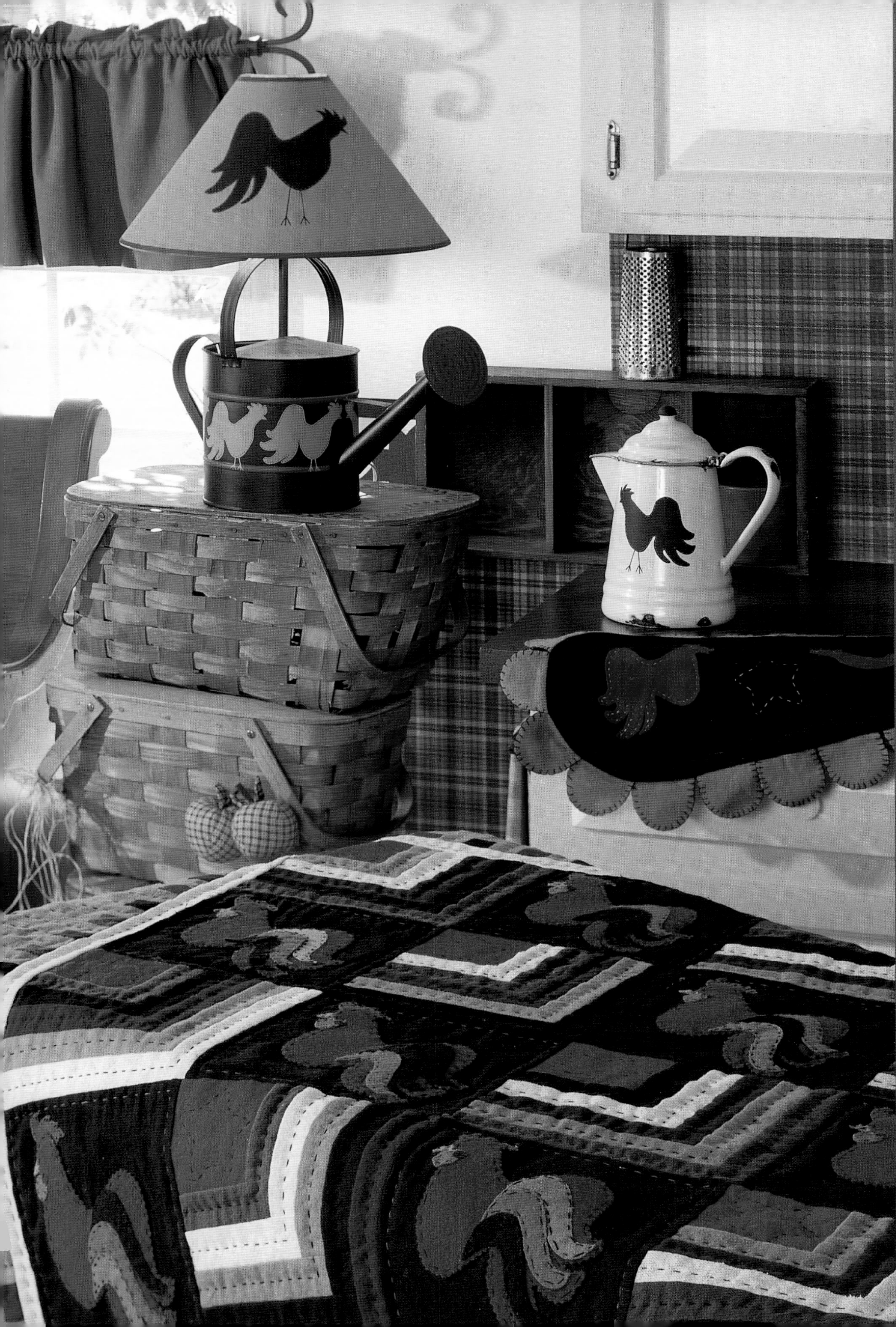

Folk Art Rooster Kitchen

If primitive is your preference, this kitchen will have you crowing with delight. Rooster motifs take center stage on a background of muted colors, while felted wool adds a hint of texture. To experience a taste of the time period that inspired this setting, make your own felted wool. Purchase 100 percent–wool fabric in the color desired, machine wash in the hottest water available (you can also boil the fabric in a pot of water on top of the stove), then machine dry on the highest setting. The heat and agitation will cause the fibers to shrink and compact, felting the wool. Because the fabric will shrink, and the instructions are based on 42"-wide material, measure the finished fabric width and adjust the amount of fabric needed, if necessary. If you're felting more than one color, be sure to wash and dry the pieces separately.

THE BASIC OFF-CENTER LOG CABIN BLOCK

This block is used to make the quilt and curtains for the Folk Art Rooster Kitchen. The following instructions will guide you through the process of completing one block. Each project will give instructions for the specific materials needed to complete that project.

The colors for each block will be the same, but the position of the colors will vary between the blocks, except for the corner square, which will always be red. For each block, cut the two strips that run perpendicular to each other from the same fabric. For instance, cut strips #1 and #2 from olive, strips #3 and #4 from black, and so on until all five of the block fabrics are used. If you are making more than one block, rotate the fabric positions as desired.

As with the Log Cabin block, the many pieces required to make the block require maintaining an exact $1/4$"-wide seam allowance. Also to help ensure accuracy, each of the block strips are cut exactly to size. Press the seams away from the center of the block as each strip is added, and then measure the block. Adjust the seam allowances as needed.

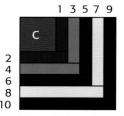

Finished block size: 8"

CUTTING FOR ONE BLOCK

From the red fabric, cut:
  1 square 3½" x 3½" (C/corner)
From the olive, blue, tan, ecru, and black solids, cut from *each:*
  1 strip, 1½" x 18"; randomly crosscut and
    label the following:
  1 strip, 1½" x 3½" (#1)
  1 strip, 1½" x 4½" (#2)
  1 strip, 1½" x 4½" (#3)
  1 strip, 1½" x 5½" (#4)
  1 strip, 1½" x 5½" (#5)
  1 strip, 1½" x 6½" (#6)
  1 strip, 1½" x 6½" (#7)
  1 strip, 1½" x 7½" (#8)
  1 strip, 1½" x 7½" (#9)
  1 strip, 1½" x 8½" (#10)

ASSEMBLING THE BLOCKS

1. Lay out the entire block as shown in the diagram.

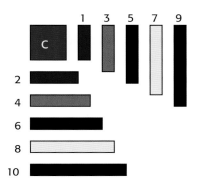

2. Sew #1 to the right-hand side of C; press the seam allowance away from the center.
3. Add the same color #2 strip to the bottom edge of the C/#1 unit and press. Continue adding strips to the right-hand side and bottom in numeric sequence.

Quilt

Finished Quilt Size: 51" x 67"
Finished Block Size: 8" x 8"

MATERIALS (42"-wide fabric)

⅞ yd. red solid for pieced blocks and pieced
    outer border
⅝ yd. blue solid for pieced blocks and pieced
    outer border
¾ yd. olive solid for pieced blocks, corner
    squares, and pieced outer border
1½ yd. tan solid for pieced blocks and pieced
    outer border
¾ yd. ecru solid for pieced blocks and inner
    border
1⅞ yds. black solid for pieced blocks, appliqué
    blocks, pieced outer border, and binding
½ yd. red solid felted wool for rooster bodies
⅛ yd. *each* of eight assorted felted wool solids
    for tail feathers, beak, wattles, and comb
3½ yds. fabric for backing
Twin-size batting (72" x 90")
2 yds. fusible web
Black embroidery floss

CUTTING

From the red solid, cut:
    2 strips, each 3½" x 42"; crosscut into 18
        squares, each 3½" x 3½", for pieced
        blocks
    2 strips, each 1½" x 42", for pieced outer
        border
    6 strips, each 2½" x 42", for binding
From the blue solid, cut:
    10 strips, each 1½" x 42", for pieced blocks
        and pieced outer border
From the olive solid, cut:
    10 strips, each 1½" x 42" strips, for pieced
        blocks and pieced outer border
    4 squares, each 5" x 5", for corner squares
From the tan solid, cut:
    10 strips, each 1½" x 42" for pieced blocks
    8 strips, each 4" x 42", for pieced outer
        border
From the ecru solid, cut:
    10 strips, each 1½" x 42", for pieced blocks
    5 strips, each 1½" x 42", for inner border
From the black solid, cut:
    10 strips, each 1½" x 42", for pieced blocks
        and pieced outer border
    5 strips, each 8½" x 42"; crosscut into 17
        squares, each 8½" x 8½" for appliqué
        blocks
From the backing fabric, cut:
    1 panel, 55" x 71" (see "Choosing Batting
        and Backing" on page 13)

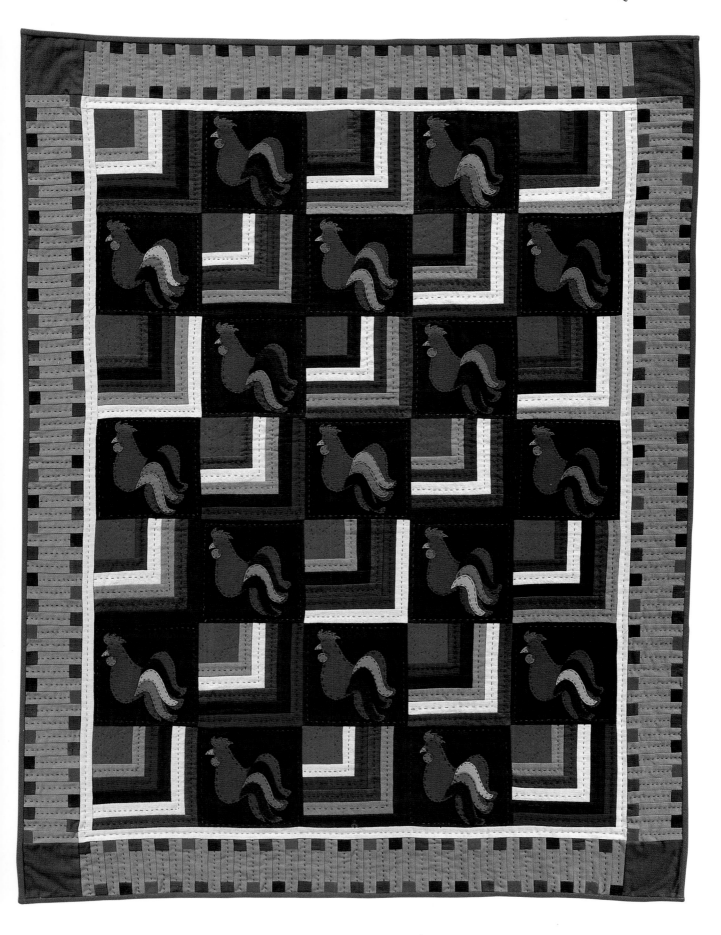

ASSEMBLING THE QUILT TOP

1. Refer to "The Basic Off-Center Log Cabin Block" on pages 80–81 to use the red 3½" squares and the blue, olive, tan, ecru, and black 1½" x 42" strips to construct a total of 18 Off-Center Log Cabin blocks.

2. Refer to "Fusible Web Appliqué" on page 9 to trace the patterns on page 120 onto the paper side of the fusible web. You will need to trace 17 each of A, B, C, D, and E, and 51 of F. Cut around the motifs. Refer to the photo to fuse each one to the appropriate fabric. Follow the Appliqué Assembly Diagram below to assemble each rooster appliqué. Fuse each appliqué to a black 8½" x 8½" square. Stitch around the appliqué edges in a primitive running stitch with 2 strands of black embroidery floss (see "Embroidery Stitches" on page 10). Make 17 appliqué blocks.

Appliqué Assembly Diagram

3. Arrange the Off-Center Log Cabin blocks and appliqué blocks in 7 horizontal rows of 5 blocks each. Alternate the block position in each row as shown. Sew the rows together.

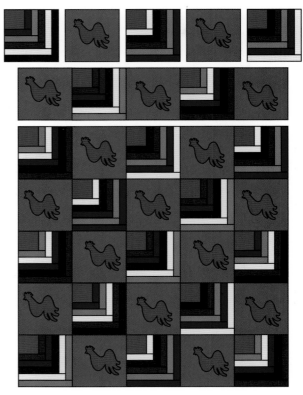

4. Stitch 5 ecru 1½" x 42" strips together end to end to make a single long strip. From the strip, cut 2 segments, each 1½" x 56½", for the inner side borders, and 2 segments, each 1½" x 42½", for the inner top and

bottom borders. Refer to "Adding Borders" on page 12 to stitch the strips to the quilt top.

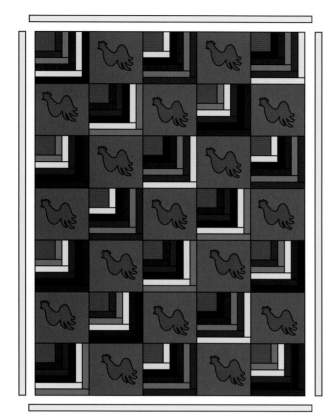

5. To make the pieced outer border, stitch each of the remaining red, olive, blue, and black 1½" x 42" strips to a tan 4" x 42" strip. Cut each strip set into 1½" segments. You will need a total of 200 segments.

1½"

Cut 200 total.

6. Alternating colors and direction, stitch together 58 units. Measure the strip and be sure it measures 58½". Make 2 for the outer side borders. In the same manner, stitch together 42 units for the top and bottom border. Stitch an olive 5" square to each end

of the strip. Measure the strip and be sure it measures 51½". Make 2 for the outer top and bottom borders.

Side border
Make 2.

Top and bottom border
Make 2.

7. Refer to "Adding Borders" on page 12 to stitch the borders to the quilt top.

FINISHING THE QUILT

1. Layer the backing, batting, and quilt top; baste the layers together (see "Assembling the Layers" on pages 13–14).
2. Quilt as desired (see "Quilting" on page 14).
3. French bind the quilt edges (see "Finishing the Edges" on pages 14–15).

Valance

Finished Valance Size: 62" x 14"

MATERIALS (42"-wide fabric)

¼ yd. red solid for pieced blocks and
    appliquéd blocks
¼ yd. *each* of olive, blue, black, and ecru solid
    for pieced blocks
1¾ yds. tan solid for pieced blocks, appliquéd
    blocks, outer border, and lining
¼ yd. blue solid for inner border
½ yd. fusible web
Black embroidery floss

CUTTING

From the red solid, cut:
    4 squares, each 3½" x 3½", for pieced
        blocks
From the olive, blue, black, and ecru solid, cut
from *each:*
    2 strips, each 1½" x 42", for pieced blocks
From the tan solid, cut:
    2 strips, each 1½" x 42", for pieced blocks
    1 strip, 8½" x 42"; crosscut into 3 squares,
        each 8½" x 8½", for appliqué blocks
    4 strips, each 3" x 42", for outer borders
    2 strips, each 14½" x 42", for lining
From the blue solid, cut:
    4 strips, each 1" x 42", for inner borders

ASSEMBLING THE VALANCE

1. Refer to "The Basic Off-Center Log Cabin Block" on pages 80–81 to use the red 3½" squares and the olive, blue, tan, black, and ecru 1½" x 42" strips to construct a total of 4 Off-Center Log Cabin blocks.

2. Refer to "Fusible Web Appliqué" on page 9 to trace the pattern on page 125 onto the paper side of the fusible web 3 times. Fuse the motifs to the red solid fabric. Cut out each appliqué and remove the paper backing. Center and fuse an appliqué to each tan 8½" x 8½" square. Stitch around the appliqué edges with 2 strands of black embroidery floss and a primitive running stitch. Make 3 appliqué blocks.

3. Beginning and ending with an Off-Center Log Cabin block, stitch 1 row of 4 Off-Center Log Cabin blocks and 3 appliqué blocks.

4. Stitch the blue 1" x 42" inner border strips together end to end to make a single long strip. From the strip, cut 2 segments, each 1" x 8½", for the inner side borders, and 2 segments, each 1½" x 56½", for the inner top and bottom borders. Refer to "Adding Borders" on page 12 to stitch the strips to the valance top.

5. Stitch the tan 3" x 42" outer border strips together end to end to make a single long strip. From the strip, cut 2 segments, each 3" x 9½" for the outer side borders, and 2 segments, each 3" x 62½", for the outer top and bottom borders. Refer to "Adding Borders" on page 12 to stitch the strips to the valance top.

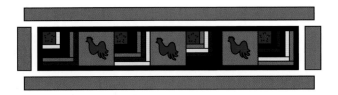

6. Stitch the lining pieces together end to end to make a 14½" x 83" strip. Trim the strip to measure 14½" x 62½".

FINISHING THE VALANCE

1. Pin the top and lining right sides together. On the top side, measure down 1½" from the upper raw edge on each side and make a mark. With right sides together, stitch the top and lining together as shown. Leave an opening at the lower edge for turning and at each side for the rod pocket. Trim the seam allowance as necessary, and clip the corners on the diagonal. Turn the valance to the right side, and slipstitch the opening closed. Press.

Leave open for rod pocket.

Leave open for rod pocket.

Leave open for turning.

2. Stitch decorative stars in the red squares with 2 strands of black embroidery floss and a primitive running stitch (see "Embroidery Stitches" on pages 10–12).

3. To create the 1½"-wide rod pocket, topstitch 1" down from the top of the valance; then stitch in the ditch of the inner border outer edge.

4. Topstitch ¼" from the valance outer edges, bypassing the rod pocket opening.

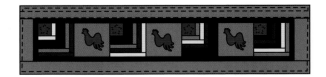

Piped Pillow

Finished Pillow Size: 12" x 12"

MATERIALS (42"-wide fabric)

¼ yd. red or gold solid felted wool for appliqué
½ yd. black solid felted wool for pillow top
½ yd. contrasting cotton print for pillow back
   and piping
13½" x 13½" square of high-loft cotton
   batting
¼ yd. of fusible web
2 yds. of ¼"-diameter cording
Embroidery floss: black and gold
Small bag polyester fiberfill

CUTTING

From the black felted wool, cut:
   1 square, 13½" x 13½", for pillow top
From contrasting cotton print, cut:
   1 square, 12½" x 12½"

CONSTRUCTING THE PILLOW

1. Refer to "Fusible Web Appliqué" on page 9 to trace the pattern on page 121 onto the paper side of the fusible web. Fuse the motif to the red or gold solid fabric. Cut out the appliqué and remove the paper backing. Center and fuse the appliqué to the black 13½" x 13½" square. Referring to "Embroidery Stitches" on pages 10–12, blanket stitch around the appliqué edges with 2 strands of black embroidery floss, and use a primitive running stitch and 2 strands of gold floss to stitch the legs and feet.

2. Layer the pillow top, right side up, on top of the batting; quilt as desired. Trim the pillow top to 12½" x 12½".

3. To cover the cording, on the remaining contrasting print fabric, align the ruler at a 45° angle to the bottom edge of the fabric. Cut along the ruler edge. Continue cutting 1½"-wide strips parallel to the cut edge until you have a total of 2 yards of strips. Refer to "French Binding" on pages 14–15 to piece the strips together.

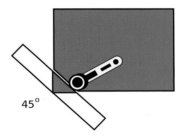

45°

4. Lay the cording on the wrong side of the bias strip. Fold the strip over the cording, matching the long raw edges. Baste close to the cording with a zipper foot.

Cording   Right side of fabric strip

5. With right sides together and raw edges aligned, pin the piping to the pillow top. Beginning approximately 2" from the piping end, baste close to the cording with a zipper foot, rounding the corners. As you approach the place where you began stitching the piping, overlap the ends and continue stitching until you reach the point where you began; backstitch. Trim the ends even. Clip the corners.

6. Refer to "Easy-Turn Finishing" on pages 15–16 to stitch the top and backing together. Stitch close to the cording. Turn the pillow right side out, press, and stuff with fiberfill. Slipstitch the opening closed.

Table Runner

Finished Table Runner Size: 21" x 12"

MATERIALS (42"-wide fabric)

⅜ yd. black solid felted wool for table runner
　front and back
⅛ yd. golden brown solid felted wool for
　scallops
¼ yd. red solid felted wool for appliqué pieces
¼ yd. of fusible web
Embroidery floss: gold, green, black

CUTTING AND ASSEMBLING THE TABLE RUNNER

1. Use the patterns on page 122 to cut the table runner front and back from black wool and 20 scallops from golden brown wool.

2. Referring to "Fusible Web Appliqué" on page 9 and using the pattern on page 123, trace 2 appliqués onto the paper side of the fusible web, reversing one. Fuse the motifs to the red solid wool. Cut out the appliqués and remove the paper backing. Referring to the photo for placement, fuse the appliqués to the table runner front right side.

3. Referring to the photo for placement, transfer the star pattern on page 123 to the area between the two roosters.

4. Refer to "Embroidery Stitches" on pages 10–12 to use a primitive running stitch and 2 strands of gold floss to stitch around the appliqué inner edges and small star motif. Use 2 strands of green floss and feather stitch 1" from the front outer edges. Blanket stitch the scallops with 2 strands of black floss.

5. With raw edges even, space the scallops evenly along the runner front edge; baste in place.

FINISHING THE TABLE RUNNER

1. Pin the table runner back to the front, right sides together, sandwiching the scallops between the layers. Stitch around the outer edges, leaving an opening for turning.

2. Turn the table runner to the right side, press, and slipstitch the opening closed. Topstitch ¼" from the table runner outer edges.

Decorator Stick

MATERIALS (42"-wide fabric)

¼ yd. red wool for rooster body
Wool scraps in assorted colors for wing
    feathers, comb, beak, and wattles
9" of ½"-diameter wood dowel
2" x 2" wood block for base
Pattern tracing paper
Pinking shears
Embroidery floss in assorted colors to match wool
Drill and ½"-diameter bit
Slate blue acrylic paint
Fine-grade sandpaper
Small amount of polyester fiberfill
Wood glue

CONSTRUCTING THE DECORATOR STICK

1. Transfer the pattern on page 124 to pattern tracing paper. From the desired wool fabric colors, use a pair of pinking shears to cut the following pieces: 2 *each* of the rooster body and bottom flaps; 6 wing feathers, 2 *each* from 3 different colors; 1 *each* of the large wattle, small wattle, comb, and beak.

2. Stitch 1 bottom flap to the bottom of each rooster body piece wrong side.

3. With wrong sides together, pin the body front and back together. Insert the comb and beak pieces between the layers as shown.

4. Use a primitive running stitch (see "Embroidery Stitches" on pages 10–12) and 2 strands of matching embroidery floss to stitch ¼" from the rooster body as shown. Do not stitch the tail feather or bottom flaps together.

5. Place each matching pair of wing feathers wrong sides together. Using a primitive running stitch (see "Embroidery Stitches" on pages 10–12) and 2 strands of matching embroidery floss, stitch ¼" from the feather edges.

6. Position the feathers on the rooster body front as shown. Using 2 strands of matching embroidery floss, tack each feather upper edge in place in two spots. Knot the floss on the body front at each spot and clip the floss ends to ¼". Position the large and small wattle pieces as shown and tack in place in the same manner as the wing feathers.

7. Drill a hole in the center of the wood block. Sand the dowel rod and block if necessary. Paint the wood pieces, let dry, then sand to create a primitive, worn look.

8. Stuff the rooster lightly with fiberfill. Insert the dowel into the body through the bottom flap opening. Use 2 strands of matching embroidery floss and a primitive running stitch (see "Embroidery Stitches" on pages 10–12) to stitch the flaps together around the dowel.

9. Place a small amount of glue into the wood block's drilled hole and insert the dowel.

Tote Bag

Finished Tote Bag Size: 20" x 20"

MATERIALS (42"-wide fabric)

½ yd. of tan solid
½ yd. of blue solid
½ yd. of green solid
¼ yd. of red solid
1 yd. of fabric for lining
22" x 44" rectangle of batting
½ yd. of fusible web

CUTTING

From the tan solid, cut:
    1 square, 12½" x 12½", for bag center
    1 strip, 5½" x 20½", for pieced back
From the blue solid, cut:
    2 strips, each 1½" x 12½", for inner side
        borders
    2 strips, each 1½" x 14½", for inner top
        and bottom borders
    1 strip, 5½" x 20½", for pieced back
From the green solid, cut:
    2 strips, each 3½" x 14½", for outer side
        borders
    2 strips, each 3½" x 20½", for outer top
        and bottom borders
    2 strips, each 6" x 10½", for handles
    1 strip, 5½" x 20½", for pieced back
From the red solid, cut:
    1 strip, 5½" x 20½", for pieced back
From the lining fabric, cut:
    2 squares, each 20½" x 20½"
    1 square, 9½" x 9½", for lining pocket
From the batting, cut:
    2 squares, each 20½" x 20½"

ASSEMBLING THE TOTE BAG

1. Refer to "Adding Borders" on page 12 to
    stitch the inner, then outer borders to the
    tan 12½" x 12½" square.

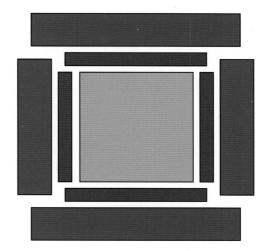

2. Referring to "Fusible Web Appliqué" on
    page 9 and using the patterns on pages 121
    and 125, trace 1 of each appliqué onto the
    paper side of the fusible web. If you want
    the roosters to face each other as shown in
    the photo, reverse the pattern on page 121.
    Fuse the motifs to the red solid fabric. Cut
    out the appliqués and remove the paper
    backing. Referring to the photo for place-
    ment, fuse the appliqués to the bag front.
    Machine stitch around the appliqués using
    a buttonhole stitch.
3. Lay the pieced top, right side up, on a bat-
    ting square and quilt the layers together as
    desired (see "Quilting" on page 14).

4. To make the pieced back, stitch the tan, blue, green, and red 5½" x 20½" strips together along the long edges. Lay the pieced back, right side up, on the remaining batting square. Baste along the outer edges.

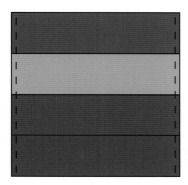

5. Pin the pieced back and pieced top right sides together. Stitch the front to the back along the side and bottom edges. Turn the bag to the right side, and press.

6. Press each 6" x 10½" handle strip in half lengthwise, wrong sides together. Open the strip and press the raw edges to the center crease. Press the strip in half lengthwise again along the center crease. Topstitch along the long edges.

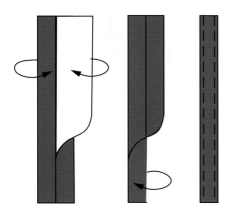

7. Position the handles on the right sides of the bag front and back 5½" from each side seam. Align the handle raw edges with the bag raw upper edges. Baste the handles in place.

8. Press under one edge of the 9½" lining pocket square ¼", then press under again 1" to create a hem. Topstitch close to the first pressed-under edge. Press under the remaining edges ¼". Center the pocket on the right side of one of the lining squares 5" from the top. Topstitch the pocket to the lining along the side and lower edges.

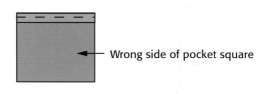

Wrong side of pocket square

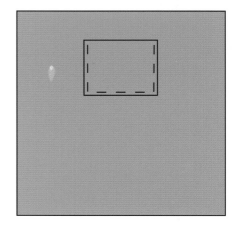

9. Stitch the bag lining pieces right sides together along the side and lower edge. Leave an opening on one side for turning.

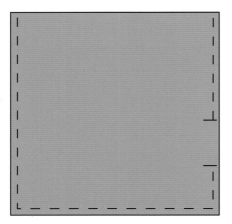

10. Place the bag front/back piece inside the lining with the bag and lining right sides together. Pin together along the upper edge. Match the side seams. Stitch along the upper edge. Backstitch as you stitch across each handle end to reinforce the area.

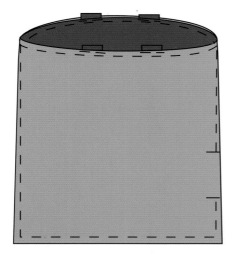

11. Turn the bag to the right side through the lining side opening. Slipstitch the opening closed. Topstitch the bag upper edge.

Braided Chair Pad

Finished Chair Pad Size: 12" diameter*

*Adjust the pad diameter by adding additional braided strips.

MATERIALS (42"-wide fabric)

½ yd. *each* of 6 to 8 assorted colors of felted wool
Matching yarn
Yarn needle

CUTTING AND ASSEMBLING THE CHAIR PAD STRIPS

1. Cut the wool pieces into ¾"-wide strips.
2. Sew the ends of three different colored strips together. Stitch at a 45° angle as shown.

3. Braid the strips together. When you are 10" from the strip ends, lay another strip over each strip end and stitch together. For a variegated look, stitch different colors together.

4. Continue braiding and adding strips until the braid is about 3 yards long. Leave the last 5" unbraided. Clamp or pin the braid together where you stopped braiding.

5. Thread the yarn needle with yarn. Wind the braid into a circle. Stitch together along the inside edges as you wind.

6. Cut the unbraided end of each strip so the ends are tapered. Continue braiding and stitching until you reach the end.

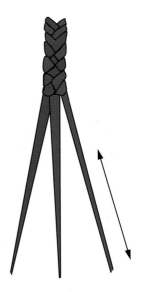

Taper ends.

7. Saturate the finished chair pad with water. Lay the wet pad on a hard surface and pat flat. Let the chair pad dry.

Floor Cloth and Place Mat

Finished Floor Cloth Size: 28" x 36"
Finished Place Mat Size: 17¼" x 13½"

PAINT PALETTE

DecoArt Americana: #DA84 Midnite Green, #DA163 Honey Brown

Delta Ceramcoat: #2406 Mendocino Red, #2506 Black, #2495 Cinnamon, #2425 Territorial Beige, #2413 Prussian Blue

MATERIALS

Pre-cut 28" x 36" floor cloth
Pre-cut 17¼" x 13½" place mat
Acrylic gesso
Water-base clear varnish
.05 black permanent marker

FLOOR CLOTH AND PLACE MAT SURFACE PREPARATION

1. Follow the manufacturer's instructions to apply two coats of gesso to the floor cloth and place mat surface. Dry thoroughly.
2. Paint a cinnamon base coat on the floor cloth and place mat. Apply several coats for durability.

PAINTING THE FLOOR CLOTH DESIGN

1. With black, paint a line 4" in from the floor cloth outer edges.
2. Using the Large Star pattern on page 123, transfer 1 star to each corner of the outer border. Paint a brown base coat on each star. Penstitch the inside edges of each star with cinnamon paint.
3. Transfer the Large Vine pattern on page 126 to the floor cloth outer border between each star. Lengthen the pattern as needed to fill the space. Paint the vines black.
4. Measure 2" from the outer border inside line and draw a 26" x 16" rectangle in the center of the floor cloth. Divide the rectangle into 2 rows of 3 blocks each. Each block should measure 8" x 8".
5. Paint a Rooster block in the center square of the first row and the first and third squares of the second row. To paint the Rooster blocks, paint the background black. Transfer the Rooster pattern on page 125 to the center of each block. Paint the rooster brown. Transfer the Legs/Feet pattern on page 125 to the square as shown. Using brown paint and a liner brush, paint each rooster's legs and feet. With the black marker, penstitch around the inside edges of each rooster and each red center square. Penstitch just inside the Rooster block using brown and a liner brush.

6. Paint an Off-Center Log Cabin block in the remaining squares. To paint the Off-Center Log Cabin blocks, draw a 3" square in the upper left corner of each block. Draw five 1"-wide strips on the right-hand and lower block edges as shown. Paint the 3" square with red. Paint the strips with black, cinnamon, beige, blue, and green. Paint strips that run perpendicular to each other the same color. Alternate the strip colors in each block. Tape off each area before painting the next.

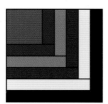

7. Follow the manufacturer's instructions to apply 4 coats of varnish to the painted floor cloth. Let dry thoroughly between coats.

PAINTING THE PLACE MAT DESIGN

1. Referring to the photo for placement, transfer the Small Star and Small Vine patterns on pages 123 and 125 to the place mat.
2. Paint the stars brown and the vines black. Penstitch the inside edges of each star with cinnamon paint.
3. Follow the manufacturer's instructions to apply 4 coats of varnish to the painted mat.

Picnic Basket

PAINT PALETTE

DecoArt Americana: #DA163 Honey Brown
Delta Ceramcoat: #2506 Black

MATERIALS

Picnic basket with wood lid
Matte acrylic sealer
.05 black permanent marker

PREPARING THE PICNIC BASKET SURFACE

1. Lightly sand the picnic basket lid. Wipe with a tack cloth. Apply matte acrylic sealer.
2. Using the patterns on pages 125 and 126, transfer the rooster to the lid center and the vines to the outer edges.

PAINTING THE DESIGN

1. Paint the vine and leaves black.
2. Paint the rooster brown. Use the marker to penstitch the rooster along the inside edges.
3. Following the manufacturer's instructions, apply sealer to the picnic basket lid.

Sprinkling Can Lamp

PAINT PALETTE

DecoArt Americana: #DA 163 Honey Brown
Delta Ceramcoat: #2495 Cinnamon, #2506
Black, Metal Primer

MATERIALS

Galvanized watering can
Purchased lampshade with clip that fits water-
    ing can
.01 black permanent marker
Matte acrylic sealer

SURFACE PREPARATION

1. Wash the watering can with a 50 percent
   vinegar/50 percent water mixture. Rinse
   with clean water; dry with a clean cloth.
2. Follow the metal primer instructions to
   prime the watering can outer surface.

PAINTING THE DESIGNS

1. Paint the top and bottom trim edges of the
   lampshade with cinnamon paint. Center
   and transfer the pattern on page 125 to
   the lampshade. Paint the rooster black.
   Penstitch the rooster inner edges with
   brown paint.

2. Paint a black base coat on the watering can
   body and spout. Paint a cinnamon base coat
   on the sprinkler head, handle, and body
   rims. Using the pattern on page 123, transfer six roosters to the watering can body in
   the area between the body rims. Paint the
   roosters brown. Penstitch the rooster inner
   edges with the marker.

3. Follow the manufacturer's instructions to
   apply several coats of sealer to the watering
   can painted surface.

Mason Jar Lamp

PAINT PALETTE

DecoArt Americana: #DA 163 Honey Brown
Delta Ceramcoat: #2495 Cinnamon, #2506 Black

MATERIALS

Lamp kit and lampshade
.03 black permanent marker
Matte acrylic sealer
Decorative dried material for layering

SURFACE PREPARATION

1. Paint a cinnamon base coat on the lampshade.
2. Using the Large Star and Vine patterns on pages 123 and 125, transfer a star and vine to each side of the lampshade.

PAINTING AND SEALING THE DESIGN

1. Paint the stars brown. Paint the vine black.
2. Penstitch the star inner edges with the marker.
3. Follow the manufacturer's instructions to apply sealer to the painted surface.

ASSEMBLING THE LAMP

1. Follow the manufacturer's instructions to assemble the lamp.
2. Layer the dried materials around the electrical fixtures inside the jar.

Kitchen Completers

With a few quick fabric or paint changes, these projects are easily adaptable to any of the kitchen themes in this book.

Chenille Rug

Chenille rugs are a fun and easy way to complete your coordinated kitchen decor. Depending on the size of the rug, you may even be able to use up the larger left-over fabric pieces. Chenille is made up of seven to eight layers of unwashed fabric that are quilted together at a 45° angle to the straight of grain. Once the layers are quilted, all but the bottom two base layers are slashed through the channels that were created when the fabrics were quilted. The piece is then washed and dried, and the combination of shrinking and fraying makes chenille. Quilting cotton, cotton flannel, and rayon are all good candidates for this technique. Experiment with fabric colors and layering order before beginning by making 5" samples of the stacked, stitched, and cut fabrics you have selected. Be sure to wash and dry each sample so you can preview the results before making the final project.

GENERAL MATERIALS

7 or 8 cotton or rayon fabric pieces 3" larger than desired rug size
Binding fabric as needed

GENERAL CHENILLE INSTRUCTIONS

1. Cut the chenille and base fabric layers 3" larger than the finished rug size.
2. Lay one base fabric piece right side down. Place the remaining base fabric over the first, right side up. Layer the remaining fabric pieces over the base fabrics, right side up, in the order determined by the sample block. Press the fabrics after each addition.

3. Pin the layers together. Space the pins about 6" apart, keeping the fabric edges even.

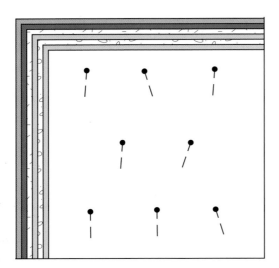

4. Draw a line at a 45° angle to the straight grain. Continue to draw lines parallel to the first line, leaving ½" between lines. Using a size 90/14 needle and a long stitch length, stitch along the drawn lines. Reverse the stitching direction for each line.

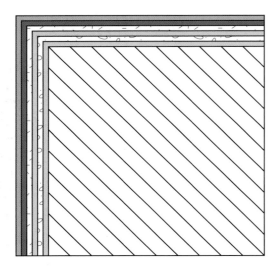

5. Cut between the stitching lines, cutting all but the base layers. There are special tools available that will make cutting easier, but a pair of sharp scissors will work.

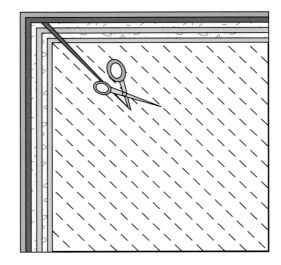

6. Machine baste around the outside edges of the rug. Place the rug in the washing machine by itself. Set the machine for a short cycle, regular or delicate, with a warm wash and cold rinse. Dry the piece by itself in the dryer at a medium setting.

7. Square the rug to size after washing and drying.

8. Measure the perimeter of the rug, and cut enough 2½"-wide strips from the desired fabric to bind the rug. Bind the rug edges with French binding (see "Finishing the Edges" on pages 14–15).

Vinyl Place Mats

These easy-care place mats are quick to make and quick to clean. Just wipe them with a damp cloth and they're ready for the next meal! Use two layers of a cotton fabric that coordinates with your kitchen theme, or have twice the fun and use two different fabrics. Fabric yardages will be determined by the place mat size and quantity. For ease in stitching, use a long stitch length and a size 70/10 sewing machine needle. Use a Teflon presser foot so the vinyl material will feed smoothly through the machine.

MATERIALS

Existing place mat for pattern
Cotton fabric twice as large as existing place mat for each place mat desired
Vinyl material twice as large as existing place mat for each place mat desired
Bias tape

VINYL PLACE MATS INSTRUCTIONS

1. Make a pattern by tracing around an existing place mat.
2. For each place mat, cut 2 pieces *each* from the cotton fabric and vinyl.
3. Layer the cotton place mat pieces, wrong sides together. Sandwich the cotton layers between the two vinyl layers. Pin the layers together.
4. Bind the edges with bias tape.

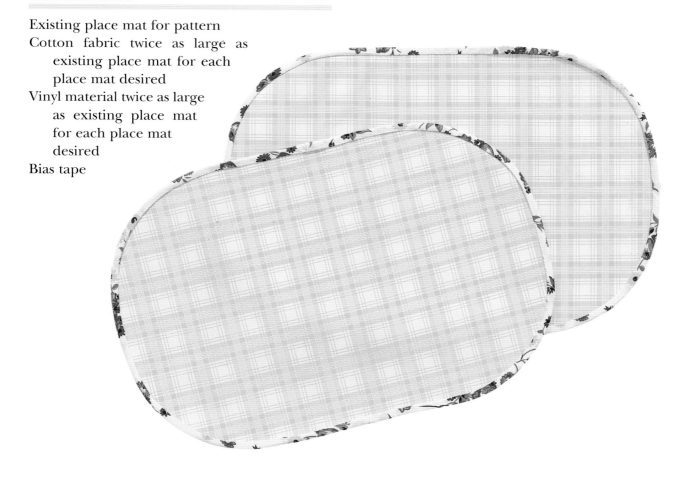

Wastebasket and Lamp

What kitchen couldn't use an extra wastebasket or some additional lighting? These coordinated accents offer functionality as well as decorator appeal, and can be made from existing or newly purchased pieces.

MATERIALS

Wastebasket and/or lamp of your choice
Fabric to cover wastebasket and/or lamp
Pattern tracing paper
Double-sided adhesive
Coordinating acrylic paint

DECORATING THE WASTEBASKET AND/OR LAMP

1. Trace the project surface onto pattern tracing paper.
2. Follow the manufacturer's instructions to fuse the desired fabric to the double-sided adhesive.
3. Transfer the pattern to the fused fabric and cut out.
4. Follow the manufacturer's instructions to fuse the cut-out piece to the wastebasket or lamp surface.
5. If desired, paint any exposed edges with coordinating acrylic paint, and fuse a matching fabric motif to the lampshade.

Resources

Tea Towels

Wimpole Street Creations tea towels can often be found at your local crafts store. If you cannot find them, contact:
Barrett House
PO Box 540585
North Salt Lake, UT 84054-0585
Phone: (801) 299-0700

Batting

Warm & Natural needlepunch cotton batting
The Warm Company
954 E. Union St.
Seattle, WA 98122
Phone: (800) 234-WARM or
(206) 320-9276
Fax: (206) 320-0974
www.warmcompany.com

Fusible web

I use both *Steam-A-Seam 2* and *HeatnBond Lite.* It's a matter of individual preference. *PEELnSTICK* is a double-sided adhesive.

Steam-A-Seam 2
The Warm Company
954 E. Union St.
Seattle, WA 98122
Phone: (800) 234-WARM or (206) 320-9276
Fax: (206) 320-0974
www.warmcompany.com

HeatnBond Lite and PEELnSTICK
Therm O Web
770 Glenn Ave.
Wheeling, IL 60090
Phone: (800) 323-0799
Fax: (847) 520-0025
www.thermoweb.com

Embroidery Floss

DMC embroidery floss
The DMC Corporation
10 Port Kearny
South Kearny, NJ 07032
Phone (973) 589-0606
Fax: (973) 589-8931
www.dmc-usa.com

Canvas Floor Cloth and Place Mat

Kreative Kanvas
Foss Manufacturing Co.
380 Lafayette Road
Hampton, NH 03843
Phone: (800) 292-7900
Fax: (603) 929-6180
www.kuninfelt.com

Acrylic Paint

We use three brands of acrylic paints, and all are generally available in local craft stores. However, the source of supply is an excellent reference point for specific questions or problems.

Americana
DecoArt
PO Box 386
Stanford, KY 40484
Phone: (800) 477-8478
Fax: (606) 365-9739
www.decoart.com

Ceramcoat
Delta Technical Coatings, Inc.
2550 Pellissier Place
Whittier, CA 90601
Phone: (800) 423-4135
Fax: (562) 695-5157
www.deltacrafts.com

FolkArt
Plaid Enterprises
3225 Westech Drive
Norcross, GA 30091
Phone: (800) 842-4197
Fax: (678) 291-8384
www.plaidonline.com

Decorative Painting Brushes

Loew-Cornell, Inc.
563 Chestnut Ave.
Teaneck, NJ 07666-2490
Phone: (201) 836-7070
Fax: (201) 836-8110
www.loew-cornell.com

Ceramic Canisters

Mr. & Mrs. of Dallas, Inc.
8428 Highway 121 North
Melissa, TX 75454
Phone: (800) 878-7258
Fax: (972) 837-4104
www.mrandmrsofdallas.com

Folkart Watering Can Lamp and Kitchen Watering Cans

Houston International Trading
5000 Terminal Street
Bellaire, TX 77401
Phone: (713) 839-0668
Fax: (713) 839-0669

Unfinished Wood Furniture

Westview Products, Inc.
PO Box 569
Dallas, OR 97338
Phone: (800) 203-7557
www.westviewproducts.com

Sakura Microperm Pens

Sakura of America
30780 San Clemente St.
Hayward, CA 94544
Phone: (510) 475-8880
Fax: (510) 475-0973
www.gellyroll.com

Patterns

Vintage Kitchen
Tea Cozy

Place on
fold.

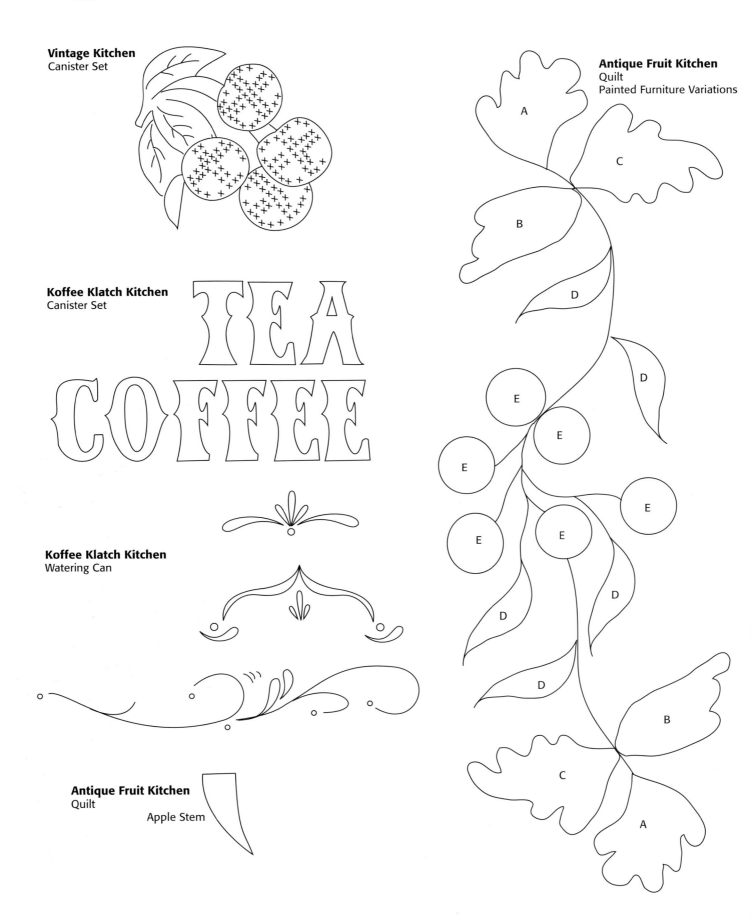

Vintage Kitchen
Canister Set

Koffee Klatch Kitchen
Canister Set

TEA
COFFEE

Koffee Klatch Kitchen
Watering Can

Antique Fruit Kitchen
Quilt

Apple Stem

Antique Fruit Kitchen
Quilt
Painted Furniture Variations

A

C

B

D

D

E

E

E

E

E

E

D

D

D

B

C

A

Antique Fruit Kitchen
Painted Table, Painted Furniture Variations

Folk Art Rooster Kitchen
Quilt

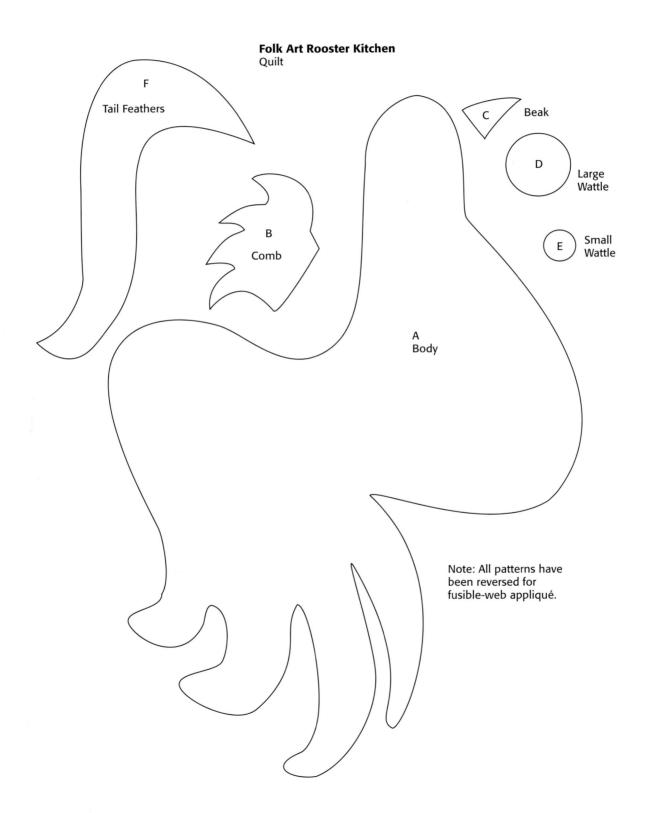

F

Tail Feathers

C   Beak

D   Large
Wattle

E   Small
Wattle

B
Comb

A
Body

Note: All patterns have
been reversed for
fusible-web appliqué.

Folk Art Rooster Kitchen
Pillow, Tote Bag

Note: Pattern has been
reversed for fusible-web
appliqué.

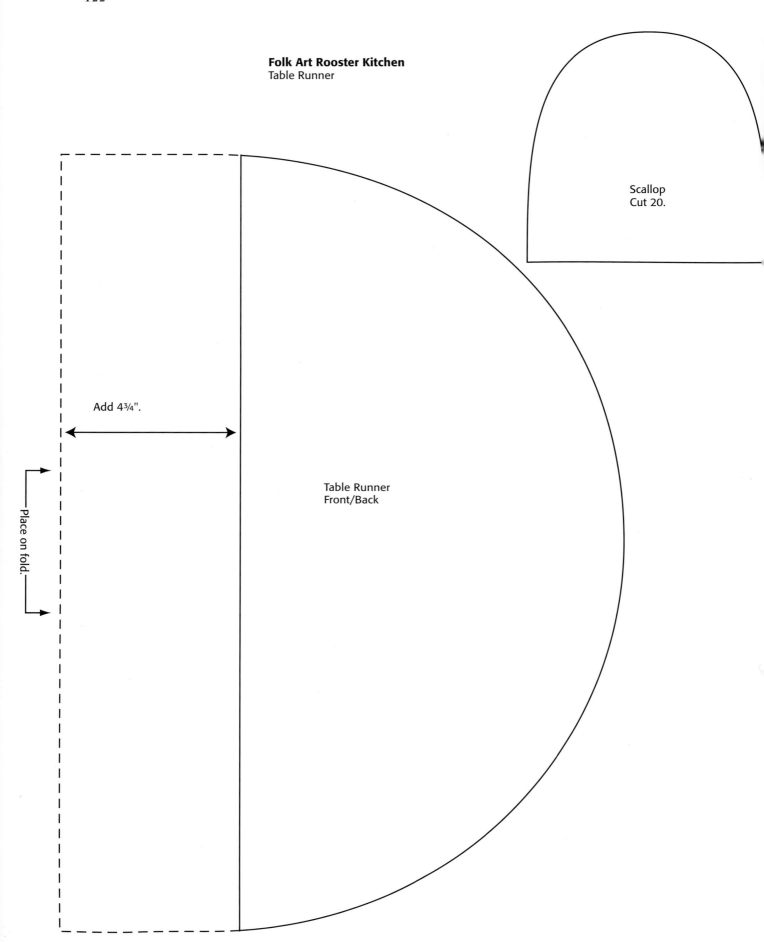

Folk Art Rooster Kitchen
Table Runner

Scallop
Cut 20.

Add 4¾".

Place on fold.

Table Runner
Front/Back

Folk Art Rooster Kitchen
Table Runner
Sprinkling Can Lamp

Folk Art Rooster Kitchen
Large Star:
	Floor Cloth, Mason Jar Lamp
Small Star:
	Table Runner, Place Mat

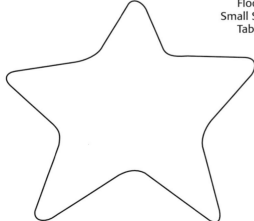

124

Wing Feather

Folk Art Rooster Kitchen
Decorator Stick

Beak

Large Wattle

Comb

Small Wattle

Body

Bottom Flap

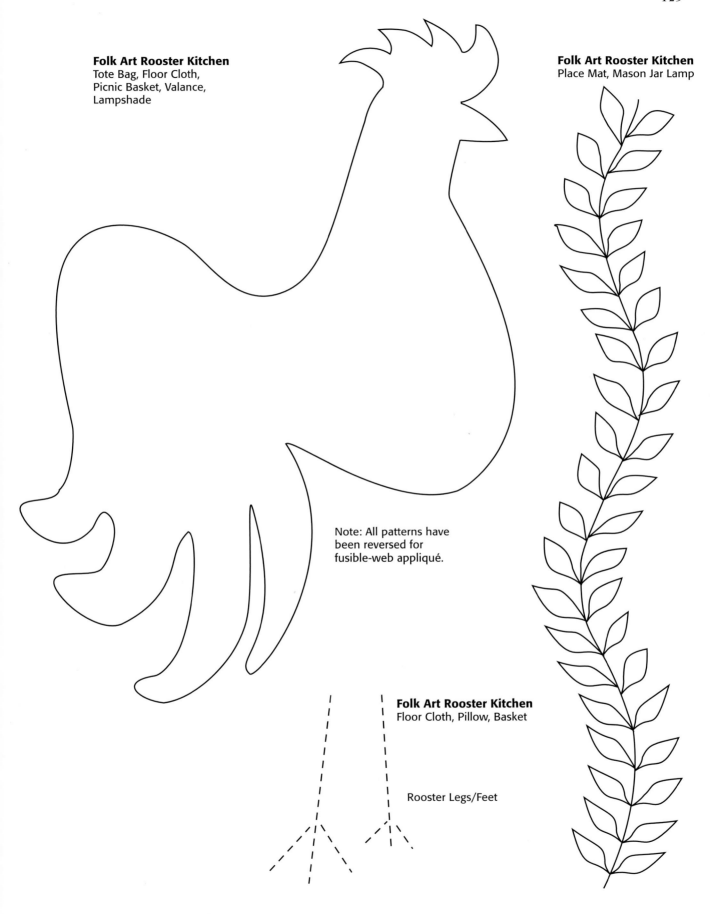

Folk Art Rooster Kitchen
Tote Bag, Floor Cloth,
Picnic Basket, Valance,
Lampshade

Folk Art Rooster Kitchen
Place Mat, Mason Jar Lamp

Note: All patterns have
been reversed for
fusible-web appliqué.

Folk Art Rooster Kitchen
Floor Cloth, Pillow, Basket

Rooster Legs/Feet

Folk Art Rooster Kitchen
Floor Cloth, Picnic Basket

About the Author

Leslie grew up in a creative, artistic family. Her grandfather, a cabinet maker in Norway, designed and handcrafted furniture. Her father enjoyed drawing, while her mother created and sold art to department stores. While growing up, Leslie and her siblings always had paper, pencils, pens, crayons, and paste, along with a healthy artistic imagination.

Leslie formed Fiber Mosaics, her graphics and design company, in 1985. The company name reflects her love and talent for combining colors, shapes, and textures. Today, Fiber Mosaics by Leslie Beck is credited with more than 200 quilt patterns and booklets. In addition, Leslie designs for V.I.P Fabrics, Simplicity Pattern Co., Bernina Embroidery Card, Plaid Decorative Painting and Crafts, Imperial Wallpaper Co., Barth & Dreyfuss Kitchen Textiles, Sakura Dinnerware, The Rug Barn Woven Throws and Pillows, and Evergreen Flags.

Martingale & Company
Toll-free: 1-800-426-3126

International: 1-425-483-3313
24-Hour Fax: 1-425-486-7596

PO Box 118, Bothell, WA 98041-0118 USA

Web site: www.patchwork.com
E-mail: info@martingale-pub.com

Books from

Appliqué

Appliqué for Baby
Appliqué in Bloom
Baltimore Bouquets
Basic Quiltmaking Techniques for Hand Appliqué
Basic Quiltmaking Techniques for Machine Appliqué
Coxcomb Quilt
The Easy Art of Appliqué
Folk Art Animals
Fun with Sunbonnet Sue
Garden Appliqué
The Nursery Rhyme Quilt
Red and Green: An Appliqué Tradition
Rose Sampler Supreme
Stars in the Garden
Sunbonnet Sue All Through the Year

Beginning Quiltmaking

Basic Quiltmaking Techniques for Borders & Bindings
Basic Quiltmaking Techniques for Curved Piecing
Basic Quiltmaking Techniques for Divided Circles
Basic Quiltmaking Techniques for Eight-Pointed Stars
Basic Quiltmaking Techniques for Hand Appliqué
Basic Quiltmaking Techniques for Machine Appliqué
Basic Quiltmaking Techniques for Strip Piecing
The Quilter's Handbook
Your First Quilt Book (or it should be!)

Crafts

15 Beads
Fabric Mosaics
Folded Fabric Fun
Making Memories

Cross-Stitch & Embroidery

Hand-Stitched Samplers from I Done My Best
Kitties to Stitch and Quilt: 15 Redwork Designs
Miniature Baltimore Album Quilts
A Silk-Ribbon Album

Designing Quilts

Color: The Quilter's Guide
Design Essentials: The Quilter's Guide
Design Your Own Quilts
Designing Quilts: The Value of Value
The Nature of Design
QuiltSkills
Sensational Settings
Surprising Designs from Traditional Quilt Blocks
Whimsies & Whynots

Holiday

Christmas Ribbonry
Easy Seasonal Wall Quilts
Favorite Christmas Quilts from That Patchwork Place
Holiday Happenings
Quilted for Christmas
Quilted for Christmas, Book IV
Special-Occasion Table Runners
Welcome to the North Pole

Home Decorating

The Home Decorator's Stamping Book
Make Room for Quilts
Special-Occasion Table Runners
Stitch & Stencil
Welcome Home: Debbie Mumm
Welcome Home: Kaffe Fassett

Knitting

Simply Beautiful Sweaters
Two Sticks and a String

Paper Arts

The Art of Handmade Paper and Collage
Grow Your Own Paper
Stamp with Style

Paper Piecing

Classic Quilts with Precise Foundation Piecing
Easy Machine Paper Piecing
Easy Mix & Match Machine Paper Piecing
Easy Paper-Pieced Keepsake Quilts
Easy Paper-Pieced Miniatures
Easy Reversible Vests
Go Wild with Quilts
Go Wild with Quilts—Again!
It's Raining Cats & Dogs
Mariner's Medallion
Needles and Notions
Paper-Pieced Curves
Paper Piecing the Seasons
A Quilter's Ark
Sewing on the Line
Show Me How to Paper Piece

Quilting & Finishing Techniques

The Border Workbook
Borders by Design
A Fine Finish
Happy Endings
Interlacing Borders
Lap Quilting Lives!
Loving Stitches
Machine Quilting Made Easy
Quilt It!
Quilting Design Sourcebook
Quilting Makes the Quilt
The Ultimate Book of Quilt Labels

Ribbonry

Christmas Ribbonry
A Passion for Ribbonry
Wedding Ribbonry

Rotary Cutting & Speed Piecing

101 Fabulous Rotary-Cut Quilts
365 Quilt Blocks a Year Perpetual Calendar
All-Star Sampler
Around the Block with Judy Hopkins
Basic Quiltmaking Techniques for Strip Piecing
Beyond Log Cabin
Block by Block
Easy Stash Quilts
Fat Quarter Quilts
The Joy of Quilting
A New Twist on Triangles
A Perfect Match
Quilters on the Go
ScrapMania
Shortcuts
Simply Scrappy Quilts
Spectacular Scraps
Square Dance
Stripples Strikes Again!
Strips That Sizzle
Surprising Designs from Traditional Quilt Blocks

Traditional Quilts with Painless Borders
Time-Crunch Quilts
Two-Color Quilts

Small & Miniature Quilts

Bunnies by the Bay Meets Little Quilts
Celebrate! With Little Quilts
Easy Paper-Pieced Miniatures
Fun with Miniature Log Cabin Blocks
Little Quilts all Through the House
Living with Little Quilts
Miniature Baltimore Album Quilts
A Silk-Ribbon Album
Small Quilts Made Easy
Small Wonders

Surface Design

Complex Cloth
Creative Marbling on Fabric
Dyes & Paints
Fantasy Fabrics
Hand-Dyed Fabric Made Easy
Jazz It Up
Machine Quilting with Decorative Threads
New Directions in Chenille
Thread Magic
Threadplay with Libby Lehman

Topics in Quiltmaking

Bargello Quilts
The Cat's Meow
Even More Quilts for Baby
Everyday Angels in Extraordinary Quilts
Fabric Collage Quilts
Fast-and-Fun Stenciled Quilts
Folk Art Quilts
It's Raining Cats & Dogs
Kitties to Stitch and Quilt: 15 Redwork Designs
Life in the Country with Country Threads
Machine-Stitched Cathedral Windows
More Quilts for Baby
A New Slant on Bargello Quilts
Patchwork Pantry
Pink Ribbon Quilts
Quilted Landscapes
The Quilted Nursery
Quilting Your Memories
Quilts for Baby
Quilts from Aunt Amy
Whimsies & Whynots

Watercolor Quilts

More Strip-Pieced Watercolor Magic
Quick Watercolor Quilts
Strip-Pieced Watercolor Magic
Watercolor Impressions
Watercolor Quilts

Wearables

Easy Reversible Vests
Just Like Mommy
New Directions in Chenille
Quick-Sew Fleece
Variations in Chenille